Happy Betw
How You Can Be Very Happy When Not Involved With A Partner For 1 Hour Or 10 Years

Ken Rutkowski

Published by McAlpine Press
Cupertino, CA
(408) 255-3724 * Fax (408) 873-7633
e-mail: macal@pacbell.net

Happy Between Relationships
How You Can Be Very Happy When Not Involved With A Partner For 1 Hour Or 10 Years

By Ken Rutkowski

Published by:

McAlpine Press
21265 Stevens Creek Blvd
Suite 205-527 Cupertino, CA 95014

All rights reserved. No part of this book may be reproduced or retransmitted in any form or by any means, electronic or mechanical, including photocopying, recording or by any information storage and retrieval system without written permission from the author, except for the inclusion of brief quotations in a review.

Copyright © 1999 by Ken Rutkowski

Publisher's Cataloging-in-Publication
Rutkowski, Ken.
   Happy between relationships : how you can be very happy when not involved with a partner for 1 hour or 10 years / Ken Rutkowski--1st ed.
   p. cm.
   Preassigned LCCN: 98-65324
   ISBN: 0-9662933-3-9

   1. Solitude. 2. Loneliness. 3. Separation--Psychology.
4. Single people--Life skills guides. 5. Divorced people--Life skills guides. I. Title.
   BF575.L7R88 1998   155.9'2
                               QBI98-573

Table of Contents

Introduction 1

Part 1: Getting Over a Breakup as Quickly and Completely as Possible 7

Chapter 1: Ways of Recovering from a breakup 9
Chapter 2: No Regrets 13
Chapter 3: Stress can be Diffused and Used 19
Chapter 4: Hate Well or Not at All 23
Chapter 5: Love's Not Meant to Last Sometimes—So What! 25
Chapter 6: Get up! 29
Chapter 7: Become a Philosopher 33
Chapter 8: A Time to Hone Your Charms 37

Part 2: Laying the Foundation for *Lasting* Happiness 41

Chapter 9: How 'Happiness' is Used in the Media and Everyday Speech 43
Chapter 10: What is Happiness? 45
Chapter 11: What is Love and What does it Mean? 49
Chapter 12: Loving Yourself 51
Chapter 13: Loving Your Life 53
Chapter 14: Falling in Love with Your Career 55
Chapter 15: Falling in Love with the Planet Earth 57
Chapter 16: Falling in Love with the Universe 59
Chapter 17: The Basis of it All 61
Chapter 18: The Don't-Think-About-it School of Happiness 67
Chapter 19: The Price to be Paid for Happiness 71
Chapter 20: Dealing With Nature Urging You to Start a Family 75
Chapter 21: Becoming Forever Young 79
Chapter 22: Determining at What Age it is Hardest to Find Happiness 87
Chapter 23: Continuing to be Happy Between Relationships in Your Next Relationship (or the Need for Passion in the Workplace Too) 93

Chapter 24: More on Building Independent Happiness in the Midst of a Relationship   97
Chapter 25: What is *Real* Happiness?   101

Part 3: Making the Single Life a Good Thing   105

Chapter 26: Exterminating Lonliness and Boredom   107
Chapter 27: Exploding the Notion that Boredom is Part of Life   109
Chapter 28: When am I Officially Between Relationships?   111
Chapter 29: Putting the Time Between Relationships into Perspective   117
Chapter 30: Overview of Marriage   121
Chapter 31: Traditional Views   125
Chapter 32: That Ring of Permanence   127
Chapter 33: Destroying the Image   129
Chapter 34: About my Own Happy Aloneness   133
Chapter 35: Meaning Equals Excitement   135
Chapter 36: Defining Goals for the Single Life—and Accomplishing them   137
Chapter 37: The Case for Being Single: the Arguments, the Reasons   139
Chapter 38: Advantages of Being Unattached   141
Chapter 39: Taking a Break from Sex   145
Chapter 40: The Benefits for Women of Being Temporarily Unattached   147
Chapter 41: Using the Single Life to Make Sure You Avoid Getting into Abusive Relationships   151
Chapter 42: Taking People or Leaving Them   153
Chapter 43: Reinforcing and Polishing Your Spirit   155
Chapter 44: Dealing with AIDS and Venereal Disease   159
Chapter 45: A Short List   163
Chapter 46: Looking Calmly at Romantic Love   165
Chapter 47: My Qualifications for Writing this Book   167

Part 4: Thriving in the Single Life (Among People)

Chapter 48: Why is it Not Just Desirable—but Important—to be Happy Between Relationships   171
Chapter 49: Developing Your Sense of Humor   177
Chapter 50: Looking upon Your Life as an Adventure Novel   187
Chapter 51: The Benefits and Drawbacks of Friendship   191
Chapter 52: The Drawbacks of Friendship   197
Chapter 53: Developing (or Repairing) Your Relationship with Your Parents   201
Chapter 54: Enjoying the Act of Work More Than the Money   207
Chapter 55: Saving Money: a Solid, Possibly Too Obvious, Way to Increase Happiness When Not in a Relationship   209

Part 5: Thriving in the Single Life (in Splendid Solitude)   211

Chapter 56: Using Media Contact as Relationship Substitutes   213
Chapter 57: Making Happy Progress in Solitude   217
Chapter 58: Cultivating Dynamic Habits   223
Chapter 59: Finding Happiness When in Isolation from the Usual Social Scene   227
Chapter 60: Reading Books   235
Chapter 61: The Computer and Happiness   239
Chapter 62: The Internet and the Person Between Relationships   241
Chapter 63: Good Uses of the Web and TV for Those Between Relationships   245
Chapter 64: Outdoor Paths to Happiness Between Relationships   249
Chapter 65: Exercising Your Happiness   254
Chapter 66: Get a Cat to Learn How to be Alone   259

Commencement   263

Introduction

Why I wrote this book, what's in it, how to use it, what you should know about the author

Why I wrote this book

I know two things about being between relationships: that it is a state virtually everyone will have to face, and that virtually everyone dreads doing so.

I wrote this book for one reason: to show people that not only can being between relationships be painless, it can be a happy time and the origin of lasting joy and prosperity both in and out of relationships for the rest of your life.

Such sweeping benefits are possible because of the truly vast amounts of time even most married people spend between relationships, not to mention singles. Think about it: whenever you are not with a romantic partner you are between relationships!

For a single person, of course, there is much more time between relationships. And, whether they realize it or not, how well they use this time will most likely create sweeping results. These could be the benefits I mentioned, ensuring continual happiness—or disastrous mistakes, ensuring a continual struggle to find even a few scraps of enjoyment.

Equally sweeping developments—both to the good and the bad—will very likely be brought about for married people and those otherwise in long term relationships by the way they use their time between relationships.

The reason for this is that happiness is vitally important. It is not a luxury item. It is an essential component to your success and health

Introduction

every day, in every part of every day. Without it occurring regularly, if not every instant, during all parts of most days, bad decisions will begin to be made. The happiness-starved parts will begin overloading the better-feeding parts.

In a marriage this means the time when the couple are together will be constantly pressured to churn out more happiness than it can easily provide, if one or both of the people in it have no independent happiness. Result: the relationship is over-burdened and liable to eventual collapse.

A single person who is uncomfortable being single will most likely not have enough patience to wait for the right match—even if they are patient by nature. Result: a major and wholly avoidable mistake in life with many possible major complications, such as abuse, divorce, children and child custody battles etc.

Happiness between relationships is therefore crucial. Luckily it is wholly attainable, and what's more without major expense, either financial or in terms of time. All that's required to start down this road is:

    1) a willingness to be open to the suggestion that being without a partner can be as good as being with one and

    2) the putting into practice the techniques of this book.

What's in the book

This resource is divided into 5 parts, and each part is subdivided into a series of short, dense, to-the-point chapters full of practical knowledge that can be put to use at once to make your life between relationships happier.

Part 1 is all about recovering from a breakup. It is entitled " Recovering from a breakup as quickly and completely as possible." But it is not only for people who have recently ended a relationship. Since many people still feel sadness or bitterness about past, sometimes long past, breakups, they will want to read it to put these harassing spirits finally to rest. Others, now in good relationships, will want to read it so as to be prepared for the possibility of this—or any future—relationship ending. Because, though I'm not saying an end is inevitable, it *is* an inevitable tragedy when a relationship ends without you being prepared to handle it.

Part 2 is about happiness in general. It paints the big picture of happiness in life, what it is, why it's necessary, what it's essential elements are, and the all-important steps on how to go about acquiring these elements. It's entitled "Laying the foundation for *lasting* happiness." This of course is for everyone equally, but it also deals with problems specific to the single life.

Part 3 is entitled "Making the single life a good thing." This part is based on my belief that the single life—that is, any amount of time spent out of a romantic relationship—need not be an inferior part of life to even the best moments of the best relationships. It is about learning to look upon single time as not something to be endured but rather a time to take big steps toward self-fulfillment and indestructible happiness.

Parts 4 and 5 are about diving into the single life head first.

If Parts 1-3 are about recognizing the benefits of the single life and doing your first tentative wading, Parts 4 and 5 are about diving in head first from a platform with a twist into a somersault ending in a splashless entry. They are both about ways to thrive in the single life and make the most intensely happy progress possible toward three crucial goals:

> 1) Establishing an unshakable foundation of happiness not dependent on the way others treat you.
>
> 2) Creating an attitude toward future or current relationships which will give them the best chance to fulfill their potential.
>
> 3) Giving you the ultimate effectiveness in tackling career and learning goals.

Introduction

Part 4 is entitled "Thriving in the single life (among people)."

Part 5 is entitled "Thriving in the single life (in splendid solitude)."

How to use this book

This book exists to drive home the importance of anticipating, looking forward to, and finally using the single life. It exists to drive home the importance of not only using the single life but realizing its dominant role in everyone's life—as a monopolizer of the human lifetime. For even in the rare case of a happy couple who work side by side all day long before spending each restful evening together, there is no escaping the single life. Because every time they cease substantial conversation each is more alone than together—alone with only their own inner voices providing real intimate companionship.

And so as such, as a storehouse of detailed ways and encouragement and reminders, this book should be read—but also, perhaps even more important to its usefulness, be referred to from time to time.

This means that when you get up on the wrong side of the bed, when you are frustrated, when life seems generally drab, unfair, trivial... burdensome and painful... try opening this book and reading a line or two. Because what your holding is nothing less than mental ammunition in the war against negativism. Each paragraph is a missile designed to seek out life-wasting tendencies and blow them out of the water.

What you should know about the author

Becoming truly happy between relationships is not only not something that can happen overnight, it is not something that will become automatic once it is achieved. Like all things of great value, to get it you must work toward it steadily, consciously, daily, with all the creativity at your disposal. But you must also have a place to start and a map with a series of potential roads to your destination. You will also want a spark—or even a hot seat at times—to get you off your couch and on the road; and, once on the road, someone in your passenger seat who has personally been down this road before, who on top of this is not above

Happy Between Relationships

being friendly and even humorous and fun-loving....

Dear reader, I am this map. I am this spark, this hot seat, this friendly—at times even humorous—passenger seat occupant.

Because, as I mentioned above, I have been down this road before. You see, I am someone who has experienced a gut-wrenching breakup and its subsequent gut-wrenching loneliness—once. Since that time, early in my life, I have virtually never been lonely, never been bored. And so this book is not so much a bundle of research—though there's plenty of that, as you will see—as a bundle of personal knowledge derived from daily success at being happy between relationships.

And so what I am all about, and what I am offering you, is down-to-earth, solid, tried and true knowledge and advice. And this is nothing more than the common sense conclusions of one who has taken the chance of wallowing in the single life, opening myself to all its possibilities, frightening and thrilling, and finding that the thrilling far outnumbered the former.

Let's begin now on this exciting journey together.

Introduction

All our evils come from not being able to be alone.

Jean De La Bruyere, essayist

Part 1

Getting over a Breakup as Quickly and Completely as Possible

Part 1: Getting Over a Breakup Quickly and Completely

1.

Ways of Recovering from a Breakup

✳

When a breakup hits you are not just stuck with one option: thinking about the other person and what went wrong and what if anything might be done to patch it up—generally being sad and depressed. Though a day or two of dimmed spirits (a mild depression) is virtually unavoidable, even in this brief period of raw emotion there are ways to soothe the spirit and make it begin to hear the voice of reason. And the voice of reason will always point out long lists of good things to be had or done within your reach—if you can reduce the volume of the whining, crying and complaining of your emotions. Here are some ways to do this. (Note: I'm not saying that you can *completely* get over, say, a divorce in a few days—just make it so that you can function and see clearly the light at the end of the tunnel.)

For those first few hours after the breakup, the ideal way to battle the negative emotions is to get together with a friend who will not only listen to your outpourings but speak of their own experiences. Having a receptive someone to express your confused feelings to will make you sort out the extreme from the reasonable. Having this friend speak of her or his own breakups will remind you that what you're going through is a natural and common event that everybody has to deal with. And so you will most likely be prevented from building it up through an accumulating cloud of unbroken black thoughts to the proportions of a catastrophe.

If there is no friend of this kind available at the time of the breakup, there are several options almost as effective. One is to write a long letter to the person you're breaking up with, either to be sent or not. This will not only help you pin down precisely what is causing your

Part 1: Getting Over a Breakup Quickly and Completely

inner turmoil but quite possibly allow you to see more clearly the other person's situation. It may or may not make their reasons for breaking up understandable, but at least you will see their human uncertainty and perhaps weakness and foolishness—making forgiving them eventually possible. If you are the one who ended the relationship, writing a letter will bring out and pin down in exact terms your best and most truthful motives for breaking up. Most likely you will find convincing proof why the relationship was not mutually beneficial— or perhaps find that you were overreacting to something and determine to go back and say so before it's too late. Any way you look at it the letter will help.

Going to a busy restaurant (one that you never went to with your ex, that is) can be enough of an upbeat distraction that you will be able to sit and think more or less objectively about your breakup. Feeling somewhat like you have found the eye of your inner hurricane, you can take in the atmosphere, watch the movements and expressions of people, listen in on their conversations, order something unusual. And as the time passes and customers leave and new ones are ushered in with their new behavior and new murmuring or carrying voices blending naturally with the clinking of plates glasses and silverware, the hurricane is slowly but surely blowing out its rage and fizzling out as it nears the coast. Whether or not you feel able to write a letter to your ex, the atmosphere will likely distract you enough to produce at least a few reasonable, perhaps even soothing, thoughts about the breakup.

When some time has passed, perhaps only a week or so, a good way to restore yourself to a realistic, positive, balanced outlook on the opposite sex is to go someplace where you can find light sociable mingling. It won't be long, if you are anything less than totally withdrawn, before you are struck by the variety of personalities and attitudes. There is a good chance the point will be driven home that these cannot all be betraying monsters. Not that you are necessarily anywhere near ready for another relationship. You are just interested in preventing a warped attitude about the opposite sex. This is crucial for happiness between relationships, simply because it is very difficult to have optimal experiences when you go everywhere hating roughly half the people on earth. And the more festive the gathering, the more sociable the

Happy Between Relationships

people, the more it seems like a celebration, the better; you have cause to celebrate. You are free and getting ready for your next set of adventures—whether that means on your own or with someone or both. (Ideally, with a brilliant new love-match—if not it may be ideal in a different way.) If you can arrange it, take a vacation to as tropical a destination as you can afford.

Another thing that can be done in the weeks immediately following a breakup to restore a balanced view on the opposite sex and life generally, is to recommit yourself to a good diet and fun exercise plan. The tendency when a breakup occurs is to languish in a state of extreme eating, either too much or too little. This lethargic condition only exaggerates any resentment you may be feeling toward the opposite sex, and deepens any feelings of low self-worth that may have resulted from the breakup. Besides the less attractive body that soon becomes a reality, this is also a good way to establish a trend of being semi-functional in all areas of life—which could easily become a nasty habit, nastier to break.

When you eat and exercise reasonably after a breakup, even if it is only moderately reasonably, even if it is little more than a token effort to do so, you make it possible to defy the depression attempting to prey on you. You've heard the phrase "inner child" no doubt. Well I believe there are stouter mind-dwellers as well. And when you E & E I believe you are calling out of hibernation your "inner grizzly", who is gung ho to devour your negative feelings. The physical energy, which knows no negativism, supplied to you by the eating of proper levels of balanced nutrients, the endorphins and hot surging of blood through the system provided by vigorous exercise, is enough to wake the most soundly sleeping bear, believe me. And even if you can't bring yourself to give more than a token effort, the bear may still stir and perhaps roll over—and it's hard not to be stirred yourself when a grizzly stirs.

Part 1: Getting Over a Breakup Quickly and Completely

I hold it true, with him who sings...that man may rise on the stepping stones of his dead self to higher things.

—Alfred Lord Tennyson, poet

Every beginning is hard.

—German proverb

2.

No Regrets

"What's done cannot be undone," said wicked old Lady Macbeth. An excellent outlook in most situations, unfortunately for the Macbeths not quite good enough when your guilt springs from having murdered a benevolent king for his crown. Since the problems of people who find themselves between relationships do not usually include foul murders, they may want to consider the usefulness of this attitude. Because, after all, it is the final word on past mistakes. I mean when every other way of trying to see your conduct in a given situation as justified fail miserably—then this formula of that charming Scottish queen may be your ticket. But let's consider a less extreme scenario first.

A more typical chain of events leading up to someone finding themselves between relationships would contain faults on both sides. It might go something like this. David and Wendy had been going out for about a year. Recently a coolness had entered into Wendy's manner which had always been open and affectionate when she was with David. The relationship soon is terminated by Wendy with passionate accusations of cheating. Let's take a look at some scenarios as the possible cause of this end.

If this cheating is true, there are several likely causes. Among these that David had become bored with sex with the same person; that he'd been cheating all along; that he was retaliating for Wendy's cheating or assumed cheating. If it is not true, it might mean: that Wendy has heard David is a notorious flirt bordering on sexual harassment at his job and assumes he must be cheating; that Wendy has met somebody more attractive in every way than David and is using a false charge as an

Part 1: Getting Over a Breakup Quickly and Completely

excuse to breakup; that Wendy is tired of David's lack of discipline, which keeps causing him to lose jobs, and is using a false charge to breakup.

Many of these scenarios can of course be reversed, with David making the claim of cheating to breakup and so on, so this is no comment on male and female natures. However what I am about to say about some of the above behavior is intended to be a strong comment on the nature of relationships.

Take for a start the two seemingly indefensible cases of real cheating on the part of David. There is no excuse for cheating, right? None that I can think of would justify it, certainly. And yet is it *entirely* David's fault, if he indeed cheated, that Wendy wasted a year with him only to be slapped in the face at the end? I don't think so. If David had been cheating all along he was a deceiving bastard it's true; but there is certainly no way Wendy without playing all three monkeys simultaneously could have been unaware of it.

If David had cheated through sexual boredom, then it is possible the relationship may have been headed for an eventual breakup all along, because of a mediocre connection of minds or perhaps the time and circumstances just weren't right for marriage. In the first case Wendy might never have got into a serious relationship with David if she had used her eyes when he was around other women. In the second she might have planned on only a short term relationship with David when she realized they had a mainly physical attraction for each other, or that David wasn't likely to be settling down for several years because of circumstances such as being very young or not established in a career.

In the scenarios where Wendy is pretending to have caught David cheating, is David *entirely* free from fault? On the surface, where Wendy is leaving him because she has found a more attractive man, there seem to be no black marks on David's side of the chart. And yet it is likely there are.

Just as in the scenario where David cheats on Wendy because of loss of interest sexually, David is being dumped because a deep mental bond

Happy Between Relationships

was incapable of being established between David and Wendy. Such a connection of minds would have made David more attractive than any physical or material allurements can, and so have made it impossible for Wendy to breakup for this reason. David's fault in the matter was not to have seen, or not to have cared, that the relationship was based on physical attraction—and destined to end when the spell was broken by either a new and stronger spell or simply the passing of time. And of course in the second pretending scenario, where Wendy wants out because of David's lack of ability to hold a job, Wendy is justified in leaving him, though not in accusing him of doing something he didn't do.

So there are accusations at the end of relationships that range widely regarding their truthfulness and motivation. Sometimes one member of the couple is truly mostly to blame for the breakup, where this person may have done a terrible wrong to the other, who may have played the passive victim. Sometimes both people did a series of things to injure and eventually put the relationship out of commission. Sometimes a terrible misunderstanding ends it. Whatever the cause of the end of a relationship, whether it was a good healthy or abusive unhealthy relationship, whether it ended before it should have or way after, there is no need to regret when it ended or how or why it ended. As in the case of Wendy and David, there is always a serious error in judgment committed by both partners in even the most lopsided abusive relationships. The abuser cannot abuse without somebody who gives their consent to the abuse.

Most relationships, however, do not feature extreme regular abuse. In most relationships the crimes committed are not punishable by law. Nor should they be punishable by yourself against yourself with gnawing regrets. The person who ends a bad relationship badly and then sets out on the period between relationships loaded with regret damns himself or herself in a variety of ways. He or she will:

- not give new people a realistic evaluation as to how well they match him or her;
- waste time;

Part 1: Getting Over a Breakup Quickly and Completely

- weaken their efforts to do anything except regret;
- see the world a shade darker than it really is;
- give relationships more than their proper weight, given their built-in changeability.

First and worst, this person is bound to stew in these powerful negative emotions, torturing herself or himself continually day after day. This in turn makes it almost impossible to concentrate on even common tasks enough to do them well, let alone to think about and set exciting goals and pursuits. On top of that there is a real chance of making yourself sick—a near certainty of catching colds and flu and a good shot at planting the seeds of some nasty diseases like ulcers and even cancer. The inevitable end result is a depression of a greater or lesser degree, which even in small amounts works well for killing off all initiative, all your creative ideas, some of yourself, and any inkling you may have had that life is or may possibly be in the future worth living. And of course you come to tremble at even the thought of a new relationship. What's more, it doesn't have to end. The initial cause of depression can in time fade and the depression detach itself from its old anchorage and become, in psychologist Penelope Russianoff's words the "free-floating" variety.

The outlook required as a basis for a happy life between relationships and a hopeful future is one which flatly excludes regret: it focuses on what is practical. How is this to be achieved? A good start would be to acknowledge anything that you feel was regrettable in the relationship, on both your part and the other person's. You might make a list, actually write it out. Then go over the list and determine which are the items on which you can take positive practical action to remedy today. If there is a reasonable something immediately to be done, such as returning your ex's radio, taken out of anger, then immediately do it. If anything you think of involves extreme self-sacrifice or self-destruction, you're on the wrong track because punishing yourself does the other person no real good or harm. Killing yourself, for example, to make a person anguish over the way they treated you may work—but the effect subsides over time, and sometimes little or no time through the use of ready rationalizations.

Happy Between Relationships

If after carefully going over the list you can find no method of practical action for setting all to rights, then the next practical step is to tear up the list and make a new one. Fed up with considering items you have no control over, you begin a list of items you have total control over. Making practical use of the old obsessive energy formerly bound up in the old list, you transform obsessive regret into determined aspirations for yourself in future relationships. You use the last dying echoes of the old thoughts of regret to form a new list—actually writing it out is always a good idea—of the ways you will treat and be treated in your next relationship.

Part 1: Getting Over a Breakup Quickly and Completely

I never saw a wild thing sorry for itself.

—D.H. Lawrence, novelist

Expiring for love is beautiful but stupid.

—Jenny Holzer, writer

Welcome, O life! I go to encounter for the millionth time the reality of experience...

—James Joyce, novelist

3.

Stress Can be Diffused and Used

※

Stress is something that can be with you in any sort of job or family circumstance or relationship—or it can be almost nonexistent regardless of life situation. What is required to arrive at the latter state is the ability to look at the immediate cause of stress in the context of the big picture. If a breakup or deadline is menacing, what is needed to begin liberating you from this anxiety is a quick glance to whatever general facts about your life which are persistently pleasing. These facts could be less than spectacular, such as your attractive hair or your happy childhood, or the fact that you're passed your unhappy childhood, that you're alive and healthy, or even that you're unhealthy but still alive. Even if you don't have confidence in your ability to get over a breakup quickly, this reminder that you are essentially a lucky person, as we all are, will deal a blow to stress. And so you will see that an approaching or recent breakup is hardly tragic. And, realizing this is not tragic, you can see your way clear to real reasons why the relationship can or can't be saved and whether it should be; or real reasons why once it's over for you it's really over.

So much for dealing a blow to stress. Now to become its master. In order to do this we must add to the ability to see the big picture the ability to see a delicious humor in any challenging situation. Humor, as I shall emphasize wherever possible, is truly a panacea. In defeating stress no less than elsewhere.

If your relationship appears to be about to crash into those famous rocks, don't dread the collision as though it will actually smash you both to pieces. Believe it or not, there is always a humorous angle from which to view even the darkest event in your life, and that angle is the

Part 1: Getting Over a Breakup Quickly and Completely

angle of reality. And seen from the level surface of reality, rather than the depths of despair, dark events seem much less dark. For example, when what you considered a beautiful relationship that had all the earmarks of eventual marriage has turned sour. An effort to look back on episodes where you missed clear signs, in your blinding love, that the relationship was destined to fail can give an ironic amusement, as you see yourself playing the fool. Wring all bitterness from such recollections. They only go to prove something that we should be joyous of: love can make normally grim practical adult people silly and childlike. (Of course, however, this is best when not permanent but alternating with periods of sense.)

When you have learned to diffuse stress, to dilute its acids, take whatever slips through your defenses, say when a problem has just hit, and turn this manageable amount of stress into a catalyst. In this way you make stress work for you rather than against you. When the relationship crashes take that initial unavoidable burst of adrenaline and let it spark positive action. This might take the form, at the ending of a relationship, of strong sensible kind handling of the delicate business of separating so as to avoid an ugly or violent episode; of clear foresighted thinking and good arguments raised in the eleventh hour for either making another try or giving up and moving on. It might also take the form of kick starting your energies and ambitions, which had lain dormant in the hibernation of a warm cozy relationship.

When you are between relationships sipping an initial dose of stress can also be useful. Stress, when you have some control over it, is more like a furnace than a fire-breathing dragon. Is more like:

- a tonic than a torture
- a wake up call than a collision
- a bonanza than a burden

It should signal a challenge to your brain and your grit, an exciting opportunity to grapple, not a red alert of impending disaster. Problems are a chance to fly, to wrestle, to be knocked down and get back up in triumph to sink into deep satisfaction afterwards. Even if your stress is

Happy Between Relationships

a result of the prospect of a long monotonous task, exhilaration is still possible, the only thing required being a way of looking at the job which makes it an intense and individual experience. The adrenaline from the stress will provide the intensity, your own creative personal stamp on the effort will provide the humanizing touch.

Part 1: Getting Over a Breakup Quickly and Completely

I love humanity but I hate people.

—Edna St. Vincent Millay

Experience is not what happens to you; it is what you do with what happens to you.

—Aldous Huxley

4.

Hate Well or Not at All

Love, of course, is what is to be striven after in all its forms, general and particular love of every kind. But does that mean there is no place for hate? To my way of thinking hate is not an absolute no-no. I know that some people advocate peaceful feelings and love toward everybody, and I agree with this as a general principle regarding 'mankind' in the abstract. However when considering certain individuals—child molesters, con men who swindle old ladies out of their life savings, tyrants who think nothing of spilling the blood of their own people not to mention that of foreigners—I find it very hard not to feel the 'H' word toward them. And I think the very same word might also be applied to certain lesser crimes, some of them having to do with relationships, and be of substantial usefulness.

For example, if a house-husband with two small children runs away with another woman, taking the children and leaving a note of explanation and apology on the answering machine for his wife to find when she gets home from work; when a man who works twelve hours a day at a job he doesn't enjoy primarily in order to provide the high ticket luxuries his wife demands, comes home early to find his wife in bed with another man; even when in the case of people just dating one of them cheats or brakes off the relationship abruptly and mysteriously— these kinds of actions do not deserve to be forgiven and the strong feelings they naturally generate may be put, turbine-like, to powerful use. And not negative or destructive use but positive constructive use, which of course is the only acceptable way to use it. And yet weak hatred is only self-destructive, you must hate with an angry full yet *bridled* hatred; hate well and purposefully or do not hate at all.

Part 1: Getting Over a Breakup Quickly and Completely

Here is a way that justifiable hate can be put to positive use. Think of yourself as a steam-powered train. Now what is the end result of a steam train's furious chugging? Invariably a speedy and direct journey to its destination. Let the thoughts which torment you at first, regarding possible mistakes on your part, be dismissed by focusing on your former partner's over-the-top detestable behavior. Any faults you may have had, even if they were major ones, do not supply the shadow of an excuse for any form of violent ending of a relationship. So be ready to convert any cold water from a bad conscience to more steam with the heat of your righteous indignation.

So now it's full steam ahead. But what is the destination? Anything you want to do or get done really; especially what calls for courage or the overcoming of reluctance caused by nervousness or timidity. What could provide a sharper spur than the memory of someone whom you've learned to hate as much as he or she deserves telling you that you'll never have the guts to do such and such? If that can't get you rolling nothing will. And what better way to take revenge (revenge is another action some would shun altogether, but that I think can be very therapeutic and indeed fun if taken in the imagination or in self-betterment due to being separated from the person in question).

Hate of a person who has abused you can be productive in two highly valuable ways:

1) Helps you get out and stay out of that relationship;

2) Provides potent impetus to show 'em with independent prosperity and happiness.

5.

Love's Not Meant to Last Sometimes—So What!

❋

In my experience without question the proposition most eligible to make a normally cheerful person suddenly droop at its merest indirect mention: love's not meant to last. Compared to this, talking about such savory items as breast cancer, terrorism, or the various potential nuclear disasters, will hardly elicit a batted eyelash. Well I'm here to try to reverse this state of affairs: local meltdown, if I can have my way, will one day bat at least half a dozen more lashes than the subject of fading love among my converts. Yes, I mean to assert flatly that dead and dying love is mourned too much. When it comes to love people are a lot like attention-loving cats and dogs; wanting the back and chin scratching to go on and on and on, looking up out of their sweet scratch-induced dreams with a horrified expression if the magic hand is removed.

And it may only be the case that the fiery itch-relieving phase of love has passed away, mistaken for love itself fading to a shadow of the original—love maturing to higher less sexual plains. However in many cases undoubtedly the cooling of hyperactive interest—sexual, conversational, visual—in one another signals the beginning of the end of a superficial love. And, let's face it, the kind of love based on mutual sincere admiration or enjoyment of nearly every single aspect of the other's being—-the only foundation on which to build a never-fading love—is very rare. And so what we are left with is the likelihood that you will experience fading love, some evaporating faster or slower than others, in your life and possibly a number of times. Thus everyone should try to come to grips with the problem from the earliest possible date.

Part 1: Getting Over a Breakup Quickly and Completely

It is not sad, should not be sad, I'll say, and here are a few reasons why:

- If you were moved enough by your relationship to consider it love, however briefly, you should consider yourself lucky—many people, though they try very hard, can never tell themselves in self-searching moments that they have been touched by that magic.

- The opportunity for adventure after the period of relative predictability that was your former relationship, adventure not only in the social and dating sense but in many other choices previously locked into routine.

- The sense, by itself, without reference to the concrete circumstances of your life, of sheer freedom and limitless possibility.

Say I've just been witness to the end of a relationship in which at some point I considered that I was in love with my girlfriend. No matter the trigger of this end, I will allow myself no more than two days to win the war on bugs—the stray emotional pests which, if allowed, multiply into a black cloud of locusts to darken your thoughts indefinitely. The scene is this: we have broken up at a restaurant, having come in separate cars straight from work; now I am standing out front by myself, at the very beginning of my aloneness. My heart is wild with indignation (say she dumped me), and a slowly growing mixture of fear of the unknown and the pleasant tingle of freedom. Without looking back, I get in my car and go straight home, realizing that turbulent emotions and driving mix even less well than drinking and the latter.

On reaching home I change into walking gear and speed back out with determined rather than aimless steps; walk a favorite walk until I am purged of the words and pictures of the break up scene; come home, go to bed, and sleep well from the exercise of the walk, which may have taken several hours.

Next morning get up early to prevent falling prey to the exploitation of

Happy Between Relationships

these vulnerable hours by dark thoughts; banish cobweb creatures with a dose of exercise and caffeine, reflecting as the blood begins revving up that the images of yesterday's event have already receded somewhat if not faded at all. Say today is Saturday, go then to a public place thinly scattered with people for the middle part of the day. Here I can read a good book slowly and pause to take in the relaxed atmosphere and do a volume's worth of dreaming on how I might best capitalize on the time-gift I've received. Then come home as the evening approaches, my work done, the task of applying the sealer handed over to the subconscious, and cheerfully go about a routine evening before going to a restful bed.

After these two days, dream-seeds having been planted to sprout a lush crop of motivation, all that is left for the total eradication of the few relationship-pests left with their stingers still on is the regular crop dusting of work on your new projects and goals. That is the main thing, but it doesn't mean just work in the sense of hard laborious work; I'm also referring to:

- play projects;
- recreation goals;
- dream schemes;
- creative organization of minor everyday tasks;
- whimsical choices of restaurants.

In short, anything that occupies you in a consuming, or interesting, or amusing, way. In this way your new life will be something to look forward to every day. And though the ending of a love relationship is essentially the end of a major phase in your life, the gap between loves should also be considered a major phase. The right pursuits can make it as reliably satisfying as your favorite delicacy, and this is leaving wholly out of the equation friends, family, flirting and dates.

Part 1: Getting Over a Breakup Quickly and Completely

How shall we expect charity toward others, when we are uncharitable to ourselves?

—Thomas Browne, writer

If we are to perccive all the implications of the new, we must risk, at least temporarily, ambiguity and disorder.

—J.J. Gordon

6.

Get Up!

Sleep undoubtedly is the "balm of hurt minds," as well as the " chief nourisher in life's feast," as Shakespeare's Macbeth laments when he has lost its benefits through the guilt of murder. And don't let me forget to mention dreams. "Did anyone ever have a boring dream?" No, Ralph Hodgson's question definitely calls for a 'no' based on my experience. Nevertheless, in spite of all the fun (thrills and chills in the case of nightmares), soothing, recharging, mending, and forgetfulness, sleep has its disadvantages. I will explore a few of these disadvantages as they relate to well-being, and especially that of one who is freshly unattached.

Sleep is full of forgetting. There is some good in this, but only in a very limited way: after you have had a miserable but not traumatic day (because if traumatized you can't sleep). But even here there are drawbacks. You may tend to stay in bed too long and when you finally get up and remember the misery of yesterday it seems even worse— especially if its causes are still in place in your life. After neutral or happy days, on the other hand, forgetfulness is largely a curse. The only service it performs while you are asleep is to snuff out your happiness or relative well-being, not to mention derailing any fruitful trains of thought or erasing any pleasant memories or fantasies. All this just to clear all slates and screens for the production of a B-movie-like dream. On waking up you are not returned the valuables taken from you when you checked in, like in a real world prison, but you are released mentally impoverished and completely on your own back into the daylight world.

But it is not just what you were thinking before you went to bed that is

Part 1: Getting Over a Breakup Quickly and Completely

gone or hopelessly garbled by forgetful sleep; nor is it just the previous day or even the previous week month or year; when you wake up after a night's forgetfulness you are almost wholly deprived of your life's memories, which slowly come creeping back as the morning wears on—beginning usually with a very unexciting assortment of a certain negative kind that likes to hang out in the consciousness when sleep or depression has made it a ghost town.

Consisting of twisted fragments of your past, you are sniped at by ghoulish voices and images a lot like Marley's ghost in Dickens' *A Christmas Carol*. These working by every means available (including, like Marley, chain clanking) to make you accept things like guilt and hopelessness. We must fight these malignant ghosts! If we don't, that is if we don't take them seriously and realize their danger, they can and often do expand their activities and spread their misinformation so that it echoes through the mind all day.

We must realize that anything that visits the mind in the time of waking up, and any suggested conclusions based on this evidence, is like a self-serving personal counselor to a king—he wants to turn the king into his puppet and become the real ruler of the kingdom. This counselor consists of all the abuse, disappointments, failures, and so on, experienced by you as a child adolescent and adult. As an all-too-vivid set of experiences he or she cannot be killed in memory, cannot be drowned no matter how long or deeply you keep him or her submerged, and so will re-emerge at weak moments to try to reassert his or her pathetic life.

As it is the tone-setting time of the day, it is crucial that you squelch this nasty counselor as quickly as possible after getting up. As a start try not to listen and when something gets through try to remember that it is not to be taken seriously. While preparing breakfast you might turn on the radio, preferably to a popular music station; it is good to stay away from current events in the form of news in the morning, especially on radio and television. The subject matter is always about 60 percent grim and 39 percent very grim, and its ghosts are all too ready to join forces with your own. Besides TV and radio news allow you to absorb lots of death and destruction at a low level of concentration, leaving

Happy Between Relationships

one ear available to the scheming voices from within.

What works best for me, quickly dispelling all negativity, is reading a good book, preferably by a fun-loving author like myself. What this does is force me to bring to bear most of my concentration and puts a series of exciting ideas into circulation through my brain—which have a much-needed Roto Rooter effect. After just a short session I am unconquerable again!

Part 1: Getting Over a Breakup Quickly and Completely

Years that bring the philosophic mind.

—Wordsworth, poet

Be a philosopher; but amidst all your philosophy, be still a man.

—David Hume, philosopher

It is not the answer that enlightens, but the question.

—Eugene Ionesco, playwright

7.

Become a Philosopher

Becoming a philosopher may sound a bit out of the reach of some people, but it really is not. It wasn't out of my reach and it isn't out of yours. In ancient Greece there existed a commonplace practice which has come to be called 'armchair philosophy.' It was an activity practiced by a great many of the citizens of Athens, learned or not-so-learned, rich or not-so-rich, brilliant or not-so-brilliant. It was essentially people getting together to sit around in comfortable chairs and discuss ideas on large questions, such as the nature of man and the universe. And, of course, this activity could be done on your own or even without the aid of the armchair. If you chose to contemplate such questions regularly and discussed your theories with various persons and, even better, lived your philosophy conspicuously—like Diogenes, a Stoic philosopher who shunned possessions and lived in a tub—then you were a philosopher: you didn't have to elaborate vast original systems, like Plato and Aristotle, or even write modest philosophical treatises.

There is no reason why anyone should not be able to come up with ideas on large exciting questions with at least a touch of individual originality in them. And when you do you become a philosopher. Why is it valuable to be one? There are several good reasons, but probably the best is that you eventually come to look at life—your life, other people's lives, animal and plant life—in the context of the big picture. When you see things in the big picture you not only tend to be more relaxed and patient regarding the future of your own life, and therefore happier, you also tend to be more considerate of other people and forms of life.

For example, if you, through careful philosophical consideration, come

Part 1: Getting Over a Breakup Quickly and Completely

to believe that in this day and age a person does not require a mate and offspring to survive, and furthermore can find contentment on their own, you will be able to end doomed relationships without outbursts of anger and save both of you unnecessary wounds.

Such careful opinion-forming on the larger issues of life will, if persisted in, lead to a philosophy of life. Now I know that everybody thinks they have a philosophy of life, but most people don't; what most people have is a vague system of morality which they absorbed as they grew up through a process a lot like osmosis, then laid away, neatly folded, in a chest in their mental attic. Their day to day lives are ruled instead by other things that seeped into them during childhood—their early successes and failures, the messages they received from their treatment by parents siblings and other children, and, especially, their mistreatment by these people. When faced with a situation in which they must act, instead of going up to the attic and unfolding their morality map, they quickly glance down at the instructions tattooed by childhood traumas into their skin. This is not a real philosophy of life.

A real philosophy of life is ideally a system of strong, detailed opinions on large questions worked out at the beginning of adulthood; but forming one and continually refining and revising it as new knowledge is encountered, is extremely valuable at whatever point in life it is begun. Some of the less obvious reasons why this is so:

> • Building a system of opinions which do not contradict each other promotes an investigative mentality and thus a habit of study and research—which often lead you on fascinating historical and intellectual journeys—not to mention increased tenacity.

> • It lets you know who the real you is, giving you a concrete attractive standard to live up to, which you feel is only natural to do.

> • You feel confident in your beliefs because you understand them completely, having elaborated them carefully and

Happy Between Relationships

discarded unclear and uncertain elements.

- You get a lasting feeling of triumph, having applied rational analysis *yourself* to objective questions—such as the way people should treat each other—thus showing yourself a clear path around any emotional neuroses you may be afflicted with from childhood.

And so, as indicated above, creating a philosophy of life is all about taking control of the *ideas* that shape your decisions in life. You can't be happy living either by irrational emotions or somebody else's opinions of what should be done in and with your life—including society in general, any institution, or mine. Use all of their input merely as fabrics of various patterns to be dyed and cut into the color and style of garment that suits and fits you best. And equally, since it is in your power when looking to yourself for direction, you might consider all your *own* options when things don't work out—for instance you might find yourself asking yourself at these times "What good will it do me to be sad?"

Part 1: Getting Over a Breakup Quickly and Completely

He who moves not forward, goes backward.

—Goethe, poet

All is flux, nothing is stationary.

—Heraclitus, philosopher

8.

A Time to Hone Your Charms

The minute you realize that your relationship is over, instead of wallowing in anything that could be considered sad about this state of affairs, turn your thoughts, as always, to the positive and acknowledge what steps you might take to grow from your experience. Take a brief look back over the freshly deceased body of your relationship—when, that is, the worst of the emotional tempest has passed after a couple of days—and with a cold practical eye assess the weak and strong points of your performance.

One area where most people are surprisingly weak is in the amount of personality they show their partners. This may not have been the case on the first few dates; then they were working hard to demonstrate at least a few flashes of its brilliance to lure the fish to the hook baited with romance or some other tantalizing prize. And yet when they are in the midst of the relationship they wanted, instead of delivering the full complement of their personality as implicitly promised in early dating, they soon allow the sparkle they showed to dim. They settle into a routine of non-memorable remarks expressions and actions.

This occurs, no doubt, because when people get what they think they are after they relax and, setting their new possession's switch to the 'on' position, sit back and bask in the warmth of their new comfort. The difference when the possession is another person is that your possession also possesses you; and that your ownership of this possession can be overturned by the possession itself if it is not satisfied with its owner—so you must continually pass muster yourself to keep it. And so it happens that, after a period of living with a spouse who went flat in the personality department almost before the wedding bells

Part 1: Getting Over a Breakup Quickly and Completely

stopped ringing, these human goods are discarded—returned and replaced with a still-working substitute, or just thrown in the back of the closet.

In order to make a relationship of any kind, especially a marriage, thrive it helps to provide, in addition to basic care and companionship, entertainment for your spouse. Television, books and other media can't be allowed to take over your job. If you are a quiet person, use your subtle quiet charms; if you tend to be loud, be so in ways your spouse finds entertaining. If you can be very outgoing and talkative with old friends, make the effort to be so with your spouse as well from time to time. Exploit the gifts of your personality to make your marriage or relationship something that is not only comfortable but fun, a ride you never want to end. And the more personality you learn to show, and the more personality you possess, the more fun and worthwhile the marriage or relationship.

And so, what better way to rid yourself of any post-relationship gloom than to get busy and work on your charms! If the breakup was due more to the failings of the other person than yourself, it is still worthwhile to polish your own charms, if only for the sake of a constructive diversion. Anyway you can't be too charming, can you? And being charming entails a happy energetic appearance; and if you look happy and behave happily it soon becomes difficult to keep yourself from actually being happy. At the same time this kind of happiness-pulled-out-of-a-hat is being bolstered by the fun of testing your experimental new charms on other people and yourself. As well as by the optimism for success in a future relationship that the idea of enhanced personality brings. And so even if at this point you have no desire whatever to be single, and you find the thought of being alone dismal in spite of what I suggest in this book are its advantages, it is still possible to be happy while you wait. And the more comfortable you feel while waiting the less likely you will be to settle for a relationship you know is wrong for you. The less likely you will also:

- drink to excess
- drive too fast

Happy Between Relationships

- slack off at work
- get sick
- gain weight
- lose weight

Personal charm may be enhanced in a variety of different ways (see "Developing your sense of humor" in Part 4), but they must all be the same in one way: they must involve talking. I do not mean that only talk charms, for speaking with eyes, lips, gestures, postures, and touching all may speak volumes of charm. And yet to be truly charming, and not just general signals of animal communication, they must play subtly off light remarks, all the better if humorous. And so to make the best use of the languages of the body and their penetrating, memorable vocabularies, you need first to do some groundwork with words.

And there is a gold mine of some of the most charming words in existence—in fact *all* of them, standard and slang—in standard and slang words dictionaries available at your local bookstore. Study dictionaries whether you have a word to look up or not! There is no more useful thing than a word all of whose denotations and connotations you are master of. It can be the ticket to increased effectiveness in every area—turning on your charm and leaving it on!

Yes words, as shamelessly available for exploitation as they are to everybody, can be a powerful source of happiness. And yet what is happiness? Now that you are on your way to beginning a self-productive time, let's take an in-depth look at exactly what we are out to achieve: unconquerable real happiness. What is its essence? And how is it to be maintained at a constant level through all of life's ups and downs? Part 2 addresses these questions and more.

Note: in the preceding paragraph I make my first mention of my term "self-productive." This term is at the heart of my method for happiness between relationships. It is discussed in detail in Part 5. Here I might give a brief definition for you to mull over in the meantime. Consider as you read on how much of what you are currently doing is self-productive, and how much of what is could be made more so. Self-

Part 1: Getting Over a Breakup Quickly and Completely
productivity:

> 1) producing or bringing into the outer world your inner self or
>
> 2) adding to the arsenal of that inner self to be brought out at some future time.

Part 2

Laying the Foundation for *Lasting* Happiness

Part 2: Laying the Foundation for Lasting *Happiness*

9.

How 'Happiness' is Used in the Media and Everyday Speech

The word happiness is a very common term in the English language. Even though it is three syllables long, it appears constantly in common speech and writing in most every context, along with its shorter cousin 'happy'. 'Happiness' can be found in candies, cars, cash; Macarenas, marriages, Mr. 'K'. It is used to express a wide range of pleasurable sensations, from foods that 'make your mouth happy' to those that derive from 'Mr. Happy'. But the next moment it has donned solemn robes and is being paraded alongside love and liberty as one of the great ideals. And as it parades 'happiness' is spoken of in awestruck tones— as that vague deity life is made for pursuing.

What is happiness? Is it what a trader experiences when, after selling a stock near its peak, she or he watches it go down sharply? Is it flying down a country road with the radio grinding out a favorite song? Is it marriage and kids? Is it chocolate and ice cream? Is it love, marriage and kids, chocolate and ice cream? Is it professional success? Is it doing what you love? Is it being successful at what you love? Is it all these plus a few others? Is it a different one or combination for each individual?

Well whatever it is, it isn't being single. Rare to say the least is the magazine ad or TV commercial that plays up the thrills of staying at home by yourself on a Saturday night. Nor is it politically correct to celebrate the wild end of the single spectrum in the age of AIDS and STDs. How about doing *anything* alone? Well maybe a little in four-wheel driving commercials, nothing else being at all explicit about solo enjoyment.

Part 2: Laying the Foundation for Lasting Happiness

It's kind of a sad situation. All of this 'happiness' being bantered in speech and the media every day and very little if any of it celebrating single activities. It's like the predicament of the word 'sex' in a way. Sex occurs on a massive scale every day, but is at best an uneasy subject of conversation. Periods of aloneness or separation from partners is even more widespread, in fact universal, on a daily basis, and just as carefully not talked about. While the obscenity and arousal factors are the active ingredients in the sex secrecy, the pathetic or unnatural life of one unattached are two of those in the single secrecy. (The daily separations of couples also constitute single living, but are not seen as such.) Leaving sex problems to other writers, are single people and periods necessarily pathetic or unnatural?

I don't think so. And as a veteran of long and happy stretches of singlehood, as well as long and happy stretches of couplehood, I will say this: if being alone is pathetic, at least it can be productive! And *very* happy, as you shall see.

10.

What is Happiness?

※

I would like to give a very specific definition of what I personally believe happiness to be. Not only because the book is based on it but also because a vague idea of happiness can lead people to consider themselves happy in circumstances which they should not settle for.

In surveys, if people are given the chance to rate their level of happiness or unhappiness by degrees, such as very happy, pretty happy, fairly happy, not too happy, the great majority claim to be happy with only a small percentage admitting to effective unhappiness. Now how many people do you think, of the people who participate in surveys or anybody else, have a specific concrete definition of happiness? Of a general minimum everyone should demand, and which can be reached by everyone regardless of life circumstances and luck?

Happiness would appear to be a subjective state. And yet a degree of subjective happiness may be only an approximation of happiness, a sort of readiness to be happy for those in unrewarding routines. It's my belief that, in order to be truly happy you need to set a standard of *objective* circumstances to be met before you will allow yourself to consider yourself happy in a *healthy* way. And by objective circumstances I do not mean just money or prestige—I mean:

- the way you are treated by the people in your life;

- the amount and diversity of self expression in your life;

- the amount of adventure in your life;

Part 2: Laying the Foundation for Lasting Happiness

- the degree to which you have been able to find the world and its contents interesting.

I believe being happy is being very happy. There is no such thing as being somewhat happy; you are either happy, on the edge of happiness, or not yet within shouting distance of happiness. Here I'll give my first of many definitions of this blessed state of REAL happiness.

Happiness. Happiness is all about love—not, however, just love of a few persons. In fact deep enduring love for the people in your life is only possible if you love a series of things other than those people first; what's more, the more things you love and the more deeply you love them the more powerful your love for these people will be. You may say, "What about money, what about a satisfying career, what about my terrible childhood and the starving people in the world? Are you suggesting we ignore the practical realities of human life as well as turn a blind eye to the tragedies of the world and our personal past? Are you just recycling the Beatles' short-sighted panacea: 'All we need is love?'" I don't think so. The difference seems to be that love in the Beatles song is an end in itself, while the love I am suggesting would provide a sturdy foundation on which to build a happiness that makes:

- earning more money;
- finding career fulfillment;
- taming bad memories;
- *and* helping others,

practical realities.

This is how it works. If you can find it within yourself to love something other than your parents siblings spouse children country—in other words what you have been told from early childhood you must love to be a decent human being—then you begin to discover how wonderful the world truly is. This is because once something non-human is loved you have tipped the first in a potentially endless train of dominoes. The way children experience a fascination with many things which amounts to love. These fascinations, however, are never called love because

Happy Between Relationships

that is reserved by adults for the items mentioned above. Why must love be so narrow? Why must people merely 'like' or 'enjoy' places and things or if they say they love them always be understood to mean 'like a lot'? The heart is left woefully underemployed by this kind of attitude.

Part 2: Laying the Foundation for Lasting *Happiness*

Do you know...that your fervent wishes can only find fulfillment if you succeed in attaining love and understanding of men, and animals, and plants, and stars, so that every joy becomes your joy and every pain your pain?

—Albert Einstein, scientist

I am certain of nothing but the holiness of the Heart's affections, the truth of imagination. What the imagination seizes as beauty must be truth...for I have the same idea of all our passions as of love: they are all, in their sublime, creative of essential beauty.

—John Keats, poet

11.

What is Love? And What Does it Mean?

※

Love is too limited in application by most people. For the majority 'true love' can only refer to a person that one is passionate about. I say that 'true love' should be applied with equal or superior truth to a number of items:

- Yourself.
- Your life.
- Your ideal career.
- The Earth.
- The Universe.

If a person can love the above items with the passion people associate with a 'true love' affair, then one's happiness in health is essentially assured. But it's not so easy as just doing it. For one thing most people believe they already love these things. It's my opinion that what most people feel, even for their lovers, when they claim love, is not the deep voluminous almost infinite passion which the five items—yourself, your life, your ideal career, the Earth, the Universe—so deserve. It's my opinion that the 'true love' of a person, though possibly terribly wonderful and terribly important in your life, is just another item on the list.

Let's take a look at each of the items of this list.

Part 2: Laying the Foundation for Lasting *Happiness*

Men are created different; they lose their social freedom and their individual autonomy in seeking to become like each other.

—David Riesman

What activity furthers and the love of life extols, is good.

—Spinoza, philosopher

This "activity out of love" will make him (man) free and happy.

—Moses Hess, writer, alluding to above remark by Spinoza

12.

Loving Yourself

✳

Falling in love with yourself is possible, I believe, for almost any mentally sound person who hasn't committed a crime against humanity. Whatever your background, whether mentally or physically mistreated by your parents, whether you have failed to develop any outstanding talents, whether you're not outstandingly physically attractive. It is merely a matter of first of all easing up on yourself, stopping for a while all negative thoughts about yourself; then, taking the matter dead seriously, compiling a list of actions which strike you as representing your individual personality. This is not necessarily a list of things which you like about yourself or actions that you are proud to have committed, as a catalog of such things tends to be too generic. My goal is to get you to see, as exactly as possible, what you have for life which no one and no stroke of bad luck can take away from you short of brain-damaging disease or death: your status as an irreplaceable work of art.

Many people, I am convinced, make the fatal mistake of thinking that they are or should try to be like everybody else of their age, sex, race, socioeconomic status, nation, and so forth. The worst thing about this is that it makes you feel unimportant unless they achieve some distinguishing position in society through some outstanding achievement; the second worst thing is that even if people try very hard to succeed at this sameness they can't help failing in a myriad of particulars—which, however, very miraculously, they succeed in being blind to. If you can achieve a conception of yourself as a walking work of art, something that:

- can be made beautiful;

then

Part 2: Laying the Foundation for Lasting *Happiness*

- be made more and more beautiful;

not

- just as something that is either happy or unhappy, successful or unsuccessful;

then you will have laid the major part of the foundation for happiness regardless of the vicissitudes of success.

13.

Loving Your Life

Falling in love with your life. This entails a challenge which most people would rather not think about, it being the bogeyman of bogeymen with regard to things to be dreaded in life. In reality, if faced with a healthy attitude, it is nothing more than a bugbear. What I am referring to is the challenge of learning to look forward to no less feared a prospect than growing older. And, what's more, continuing to look forward eagerly right until the very last stages of the process. There is perhaps too much emphasis placed upon the need to come to grips with your past, especially your childhood and adolescence. This, if successfully done, helps you live less burdened in the present; whereas it does nothing to calm the mounting anxiety you feel as the whispers of middle or old age begin to creep into your ears and grow steadily louder. But getting older, at every stage, should be cause to celebrate, no matter how your luck has been to that point—and for many reasons, of which I'll give a few now and more later.

Reasons why growing older is cause to celebrate

In fact even the losses which people fear are not really losses. It is commonly believed that youth and beauty fade and disappear. I say this is not necessarily so. You say c'mmon. But what is youth? Youth is not your age so much as the freshness, energy, positive attitude, and general fun-loving behavior most often seen in persons not very old. It is not at all inevitable that you should be drained by living of these qualities. If through keeping a positive attitude (I will go into how I think this might be done later and repeatedly throughout the book) you retain some or all of these qualities, then is it possible to calculate the increased value and interest of these later years?

Part 2: Laying the Foundation for Lasting *Happiness*

The youth enjoyed in early years is far more appreciated in retrospect than when it was actually passing; whereas youth retained beyond the twenties is aware of and amused by itself constantly and so can be much better guided into channels useful to yourself and others. While beauty, on the other hand, is maintained to a very high degree until quite late in life as a mere by-product of the strong interest sustained in living and the consequent high level of activity both mental and physical.

14.

Falling in Love with Your Career

※

Love for your career. This may seem impossible in the case of a great many jobs currently in existence, particularly those which will one day in the not-distant future be taken over by robotic machines. However, a job is not necessarily to be termed your career—even if this job is all you ever end up doing for a living. Nonetheless everybody can still have a career and derive from it the best benefits possible—which are not a good salary and retirement benefits, but health and happiness.

Here's a definition of your career: work which you have a passion for that is unrelated to whatever money it may bring, whose labors are a recreation that, *by themselves*, make pleasant a life whose basic needs of sufficient food rest and shelter are provided. After some earnest thought and perhaps research into job opportunities in your various fields of interest, everyone is capable of choosing a career. But it cannot be or remain just a serious hobby; it's essential that a career be something you truly intend to become professional in doing if you are not a professional already, even if you have very limited time or energy to devote to it. This is for two reasons:

> 1) to maintain the intensity which is needed to create works that continue to excite you;
>
> 2) the likelihood is born that you will become professional at it, for determination and persistence rarely fail in the end.

(There will be much more on ways to exploit your career for happiness between relationships throughout the rest of the book.)

Part 2: Laying the Foundation for Lasting *Happiness*

We must discover a new respect for what transcends us: for the universe, for the earth, for nature, for life, and for reality.

—Vaclav Havel, playwrite, president of the Czech Republic

All, everything I understand, I understand only because I love.

—Leo Tolstoy, novelist

15.

Falling in Love with the Planet Earth

※

Loving the planet earth. Again, liking or enjoying certain things about something is far remote from the state of truly loving something. In the case of the earth, the ideal love is the comprehensive kind; achieving a real love of people or nature is worth a lot, but achieving a love of everything is worth even more. And when I say everything I mean everything: from flowers to followers, dancing to dung, beauty to bawdy, birds to bombers. Now that may sound extreme to the point of being sick-minded. But I don't mean that you should delight to hear that a crowded downtown area has just been devastated with heavy casualties by a terrorist's bomb. I mean nothing of the kind.

What I mean is that the complete variety of human and natural products deserves our strong interest, in the sense that they all contribute to the highly exciting tapestry of life and death being frantically woven continuously. In other words, I feel it is quite moral to feel strongly interested in non-beautiful non-pleasing or even downright revolting things, viewed as unavoidable opposites of the things you naturally tend to approve of—and love can be nicely summarized as feeling strongly, deeply interested in an object, whether that object is a person or anything else.

Let me illustrate the morality as well as the personal benefits of this kind of all-embracing love of the Earth:

> • It provides against disillusionment and bitterness. If you can unflinchingly keep yourself aware of the existence of the bad, you will develop, not insensitivity, but the ability to expect and predict to a degree what is negative. Having learned to

Part 2: Laying the Foundation for Lasting Happiness

predict the possibility of any number of mishaps in a given situation, and formed the habit of matter-of-factly doing so, you are not nearly so liable as one who hasn't to be able to cope with them. And you will be much more likely to be of help to others, say in a medical emergency, than someone who has not studied all the possibilities and their remedies. It is quite true, the saying with knowledge comes power—in this case power to reduce the damage of even the worst kind of negative occurrence to your attitude and health. This gives greater resilience and allows you the optimism and energy to not just focus on the good but do good on a high level.

16.

Falling in Love with the Universe

Loving the universe. Falling in love with the universe is quite a different thing from falling in love with the Earth. It is harder to do, all outside planet Earth being beyond the experience of everyone but astronauts, but if not crucial for your happiness it is still a big advantage for those who are able to kindle this love. And yet it is not a wholly abstract idea which you're trying to form a passionate affection for. For all the basic elements that make up life, scenery, and atmosphere, which you know so well here on Earth exist throughout the universe. Though, of course, the periodic table is something that only a very few can work up passionate feelings about. But there exists a very legitimate way of imagining the universe so as to excite interest in almost anybody: science fiction.

I say legitimate because, since the more poorly written stuff is very silly, some people may think it useless except for comedy purposes. Good Science fiction, however, written by people with scientific backgrounds, can give one real insight into the harmonious beauty and awe-inspiring dimensions of the universe—as well as its very real potential for becoming in many places the stomping-ground of our descendants. And how can this contribute to your happiness here on Earth? Simply becoming constantly aware that there is immensity upon immensity, planets, suns, systems, galaxies, all going happily about their business in your back yard as it were, is by itself a really effective way of making your personal troubles seem very insignificant. But beyond that, the thought of the:

- endless mystery;
- endless variety;

Part 2: Laying the Foundation for Lasting Happiness

- endless possibility;
- endless adventure (in learning, imagining, and real future exploration);
- endless wonder;
- endless beauty;

of the universe is enough to make one who has taken the time to feel the fire of it all glad to be a living part of it under almost any circumstances.

17.

The Basis of it All

I am lucky to be alive. You may take it as insolent presumption, but I know you are lucky to be alive too. I could be referring specifically to having survived a life-threatening accident, because such are the combined dangers of the modern world and the ever curious, daring, and absentminded human brain that anyone past their first toddle is likely to have toddled to the brink of disaster. However, that is only part of what I mean. It is my most strongly held opinion that there should always be an undercurrent of joy in your life flowing from the simple yet spectacular fact that YOU ARE ALIVE. That it's warm drive can always be kept in mind, *however stormy* the surface waters get. Now give me a chance to show you why this simple fact should stand like an immovable rock in your mind; why in order to be *truly* happy at any time, even with wealth and the ideal partner, you must be and remain fully aware of this fundamental joy and strength; and why, no matter what, you will always be lucky.

When I say we are lucky to be alive, I mean the overriding implication to be that it is a good thing—*always* a good thing—to have been born. If a person has a disease which gives them a choice between living in constant pain or constant oblivion, it is debatable whether they are *still* lucky. However, it is my sincere belief that to have been born and lived up to the time the unendurable pain set in, that person had been involved in a good thing—good meaning that the miserable aspects of life balanced against the pleasurable, *if* properly viewed, should always turn in favor of the pleasurable. And I can't think of a circumstance which would provide an exception: physical defects such as something that might be considered to mar your looks, blindness, deafness, being a paraplegic; finding yourself in a poor situation such as an aggravating

Part 2: *Laying the Foundation for* Lasting *Happiness*

job, mediocre marriage with unplanned children, and so on. While these things are hard and to be corrected if possible they do not make basic joy impossible or perhaps even difficult. (I think it is quite likely even many retarded people experience a measure of this joy as well in spite of their massive handicap.)

Being alive *should* be a good thing for almost everybody and here are a few reasons why. Look at the little things, the commonplace things, the repetitive things in life. It is typical to view them as monotonous repetitive nothings, wearisome operations which must be performed as a kind of tax on the real goods of life. What for instance is brushing your teeth, putting on your socks and shoes, opening and closing doors, going up and down flights of stairs, even breathing blinking chewing and swallowing, but a series of tasks to be endured? In my view these actions are anything but mere tasks. Even something as humble as putting on your socks is more than a task: it is, like all the rest of the list, a landmark of passable physical and mental health, and just as important, a time to focus on your feet and feel grateful for all the good service they have done you. So you don't think I'm not serious, I will go farther. Putting on your socks is also a symbol of renewal, of the fresh clean start each new morning can be for us if we choose to see it that way.

In any small act can be found reasons to celebrate being alive, elements that can contribute to our comfort and peace of mind. Even in acts of neglect. If, for example, you decide that brushing teeth is not for you, you will have an extra ten or fifteen minutes of free time a day; and you will have the additional comfort of knowing that one day you can have a bright smile again if you want it, one that only needs to be left in a glass overnight to be maintained. The point is that if you look on most any small thing you do with a positive attitude, it won't be long before you begin seeing many more real reasons to feel contentment and indeed happiness with it than real reasons for negative feelings. And, just as importantly, you will see that any previous negative feelings you may have had about, say, taking out the trash were not truly valid, just the product of peevishness and baseless habitual negativity.

When considering the larger rewards of being alive, there is cause to

Happy Between Relationships

celebrate in the mere fact that they exist, in the potential that you may garner some of them, in the simple act of mentally reciting their long list and noting their diverse richness. How many of them you have garnered so far, and how many you might very possibly or at least have a shot at garnering in the future, or how many you actually do end up garnering, does not diminish the fact that the potential was and *is* there for garnering more as long as you are alive.

You may think your case is exceptional, that you are bound to be left out forever from getting a share of the really good things. I say this is not so for those who try, and even if it were at least you had your shots, which were exciting if unsuccessful, and can take pride in your effort. The ones who are doomed are those people who become convinced life is against them or just plain nasty. People who realize that there is good even in bad situations and that bad situations can *always* be changed with effort, those people will continue to receive the rewards of life, and, what is more important, be able to appreciate and enjoy them.

Now what exactly are the larger rewards of being alive? I think a list that most everyone, from traditionalist to alternative life-style advocate, would by and large agree on would be as follows:

- Job satisfaction.
- Social enrichment.
- Functional family life.
- Romantic relationships.
- Exploring environments.
- Exploring our own and others' imaginations.
- Self-expression.

The key thing to realize is that these rewards are virtually equal: any one may be used to take up the slack of another. And of course there are many more. However, I think these are most of the primal higher goals that are common to every individual no matter how different otherwise. If you haven't received certain or any of these rewards in what you feel is an adequate amount, I think it might be a good idea to

Part 2: *Laying the Foundation for* Lasting *Happiness*

keep a couple of things in mind. First that no matter what your place in life, upbringing, education, age, bad luck, and so forth and so on, you will *always* have *real* opportunities to experience more or even your first experience of all of these rewards. Second that even if you never receive all the higher rewards you desire, at least you had the pleasure of desiring and the privilege of living in a world full of desirable objects.

If a person realizes that there is good potential, as long as their brain works normally, to be rewarded in such a way as to easily offset any pains or miseries, then she or he will be a positive person. If you are positive and believe in the strong potential for a good life that exists for everyone, then you will discard negative elements in your life, knowing that there is always a good chance of finding a more positive situation.

So it is for the single person who is *happily* between relationships. This person has decided not to settle for a mediocre relationship. She or he acknowledges, however, the good things of their former relationship, leaving it without bitterness: there were mistakes on both sides and it was probably a bad match to begin with. Being fully aware that a good relationship is just another of the higher rewards of being alive, she or he turns with excitement to pursue one or more of the other rewards. But at the same time remaining always open to a new opportunity for romantic involvement, and confident of finding one even after long periods of absorption in other parts of life.

So having this crucial basis—that being alive is in essence a good thing for everyone—in place, making improvements in life becomes much easier. If you think that life can be good, but is not for most of the people most of the time; or that life's only chance of doing its owner good is when he or she is young; or that it's only satisfying when married to Mr. or Mrs. Right; or live by any other conditional or limiting idea; then you are not only doomed to certain unhappiness for at least a large chunk of your life, but will also have the happiness of ideal situations (that is if you ever meet with a situation you must admit is ideal, which is a big "if") turned to the shadow of happiness by finding thorns in roses you expect to wither soon anyway.

With this basis in place, on the other hand, a broad range of attractive

Happy Between Relationships

possibilities opens up. And, what is a great comfort and a great truth, if you are merely able to make the decision to change negative situations, you will be in a no-lose position. Yes, a *no-lose* position. It is true that you will still probably have to die some day (even though scientists are feverishly working on the problem and one day may be able to offer a consolation prize like a few extra years or even having yourself cloned or frozen—all of which I must confess remind me of various departments of the supermarket). But even this is part of the no-lose position I am talking about. When loves, friendships, jobs, personal possessions, come to their end, you think of yourself as free to refresh yourself with another such experience:

- knowing that you are better able, as experience accumulates, to make the best decision in every case;

- knowing that even bad experiences are interesting as well as informative, and that the only misery that can come out of them would be due to your own *allowing* them to be repeated;

- knowing that even with a minimum of these supports life can be happy, if you choose to consider it happy and live it creatively.

And when it comes time to die you can go happily, knowing that you are making room for someone else to begin a life of such experiences of good and bad, the bad only serving to make the good better for those who believe in the good.

Part 2: Laying the Foundation for Lasting *Happiness*

We do not slip into happiness. It is strenuously sought and earned.

—Adlai Stevenson, politician

Man's main task in life is to give birth to himself.

—Erich Fromm, philosopher

18.

The Don't-Think-about-it School of Happiness

There is a school of intuition about happiness, that if you make any conscious efforts toward insuring it for yourself you're doomed not to find it; or you will cause whatever enjoyment you currently have in your life to disappear. Many otherwise rational people, in fact some brilliant thinkers of the past, put away their thinking caps on this one in my opinion. I'm sorry but I see very little of their accustomed analytical vigor in these observations.

Even in that of one of the most notoriously analytical people in history, John Stewart Mill. The English philosopher, who was starved of emotion as a child, was accused of being a thinking machine by some opponents. And yet his famous quote on happiness is: "Ask yourself whether you are happy, and you cease to be so." Others, by other persons of note, on similar lines go: "Happiness is a butterfly which, when pursued, is always beyond our grasp, but, if you will sit down quietly, may alight upon you." That was Nathaniel Hawthorne. "Those who seek happiness miss it, and those who discuss it, lack it." Holbrook Jackson made this statement, who by his own definition was apparently lacking happiness. I once came across a quotation that had been taken from another collection of quotes entitled *Nitwiticisms of the Notable*. I have oodles of respect for these people, especially Mill and Hawthorne. And yet I wish I had been able to get my hands on *Nitwiticisms of the Notable*— it would have pleased me hugely to find these three quotes there.

My belief is that these sudden lapses into superstition show the *total* desirability of the state of happiness—unique in this respect among living states of existence—and particularly the sharpness of its being taken away. It is the same thing as when you know you have a reasonable

Part 2: Laying the Foundation for Lasting Happiness

chance for something really good to happen to you at any moment. How are you likely to try to think about this prospect? As little as possible, for two reasons. Not to torment yourself by endlessly replaying the reasons why you should get it or why you may not; and, even with the most computerlike brains, so as not to jinx yourself, especially when it comes to thinking confidently about your chances.

The only problem is, when this system is applied to happiness, what do you do when you find you are unhappy? Having never allowed yourself to think about how you achieved happiness in the past, and not able to go back and relive those experiences exactly as they occurred, you are somewhat stuck. Stumbling blindly in and out of happiness leads to major mistakes in the most fundamental areas of your life. That is:

- miserable relationships;
- miserable marriages;
- lapses of abuse in a basically good relationship or marriage;
- lapses of abuse of your poor children;
- careers chosen solely to support a miserable marriage;
- and so on.

For example, if you have a foggy notion that pleasure, any kind of pleasure, equals happiness, you are likely to concentrate on activities that give pleasure the easiest fastest way. These activities usually provide superficial shots of happiness, leaving an empty feeling most of the time. As Yevgeny Yevtushenko, the Russian poet, remarked: "Who never knew the price of happiness will never be happy."

Intense, lasting, daily-dependable happiness requires:

- first, knowledge of what constitutes optimal happiness for people generally;

- second, an understanding of your own temperament and what corresponding activities you need to emphasize in the list of what makes for happiness generally;

Happy Between Relationships

- and last, it requires plans to experiment with and a small measure of discipline to do the experimenting.

It is not something that comes to those pretending to be unconscious that they desire happiness, and that is denied to those who actively pursue it. Happiness should be sought with the same awareness of options and prerequisites that you must have to choose classes in school or a career. This book is all about getting focused on what it takes for you to be happy now and in the long run; and not on society's or your parents' definition of happiness, or a rebellious definition of happiness which is merely the opposite of your parents'—but *your own definition*. Formulating this definition and then setting out to live it, this makes for optimal happiness.

However, there's a price to be paid in effort to secure your golden formula for happiness; but it is solid gold, in fact a gold mine, because once you've found it just the confident repeated attempts to bring about its full realization are enough to provide exciting purpose—a key element of happiness.

Let's look at how this price is to be paid for a confident sense of what will provide you with optimal happiness.

Part 2: Laying the Foundation for Lasting *Happiness*

The unexamined life is not worth living.

—Socrates, philosopher

A winner is someone who recognizes his Godgiven talents, works his tail off to develop them into skills, and then uses these skills to accomplish his goals.

—Larry Bird, basketball player

It is not the possessor of many things whom you will rightly call happy. The name of the happy man is claimed more justly by him who has learnt the art whereby to use what the gods give.

—Horace, poet

19.

The Price to be Paid for Happiness

Do you really have to pay your dues first in order to be happy? Why not? If you have to pay them in your career in order to move up the ladder of success, as is the case with most, why should it be different in the matter of happiness? In fact your career and your happiness are quite comparable, in fact related, in several ways:

> 1) To succeed in both you need daily dedication to the routines which allow you to function consistently at optimal levels.
>
> 2) Success in both means being set for life: financially and spiritually, with each contributing sizably to the coming about of the other and each type of success occurring often in the same activities.
>
> 3) To succeed in both you need to understand what activities matter most as far as keeping you on the right road: in your career meaning the one which leads to advancement; in your happiness also meaning the one which leads to advancement—but also the one that makes your surroundings a pleasant world in which to live.

On the other hand, paying your happiness dues can be a much faster process than paying your career dues. In fact, to get the process off and rolling at a good clip, a few adjustments of outlook are all that is required. And an immediate impact can be brought about in the area of general outlook by simply deciding that you will form a determination to replace negative emotional habits with positive ones. Having all the reasons why a positive outlook is justified in a given situation is not necessary

Part 2: *Laying the Foundation for* Lasting *Happiness*

to begin with: it is enough that you realize that negative emotion gets you nowhere. (These reasons, of course, strengthen your purpose in every area of life, and are a main component of every chapter of this book.)

The difficulty, or dues paying, here lies in the toughness of a long-established habit. It takes some degree of success in your wrestling match with these negative habits to make progress toward improved happiness. Even admitting to yourself that such and such behavior is a self-damaging negative emotional habit can be difficult. Faced with having to end a certain kind of behavior that has played a major role in their lives till now, many people feel this ending to be a cutting out of a vital part of their identity. But not you! Because you see now that, as psychologist Penelope Russianoff observed in *When am I Going to be Happy?*, "Emotional bad habits are just that—habits that we formed. And because we formed them, we can break them."

The negative emotional habits that lead you to be miserable between relationships are in many cases the same which lead to prison-like relationships or cause otherwise good matches to end prematurely. Helpless dependency is a major one, either emotional or practical, and it makes your partner feel suffocated. This relationship soon ends and, being without someone seeming like an impossible way to live to the helpless person, he or she gets back in a relationship—any relationship—as soon as possible. And if no change occurs in this person, this becomes an unending cycle with a likelihood of much abuse of various kinds along the way. Others include constant anger and irritability, which lead to constant verbal or physical abuse of a partner, and the desperate need to find someone else to take problems out on when between relationships.

And so it is that in order to be able to achieve a healthy, intense, and lasting happy relationship you must be able to achieve a healthy, intense, and lasting ability to be happy between relationships. This, then, is the price that must be paid for happiness: the struggle to come to terms with yourself and your own life and the world we live in. And the test of our readiness to benefit others, and ourselves through others, is how much we benefit ourselves when we are between relationships. In the

Happy Between Relationships

following pages are many ways you might go about this.

Part 2: Laying the Foundation for Lasting *Happiness*

Pragmatism is the attitude of looking away from first things...supposed necessities; and of looking toward last things, fruits, consequences, facts.

—William James, psychologist, philosopher

Passivity is the dragon that every woman has to murder in her quest for independence.

—Jill Johnston, writer

20.

Dealing with Nature Urging You to Start a Family

A major stumbling block, even for people in their late teens and early twenties, to being content not to be in a relationship, is nature's call to start a family. Some childless women in their thirties will seemingly settle for anyone not too repulsive who can handle the down payment on a wedding ring. Needless to say, this is a mistake. And, of course, they know it is a mistake. And yet she realizes just as clearly that two annoying facts of life are creeping up behind her on silent and uncompromising feet, or rather hands: the hands, that is, of her biological clock.

A woman's limited number of childbearing years as well as a *perception* that her sex appeal wanes quickly after reaching thirty, seem to thrust her into a no win situation: either get married to a Mr. Wrong who resembles Mr. Right in a superficial way, or face what appears to be a likelihood of ending up alone, no husband no child. A popular alternative in recent years has been the temporary use of Mr. Wrong to have a child with no intention of seeking his companionship. While this seems to me to be a better situation than the former, I don't see the absolute need for a family (or a vestige or imitation of one) to give the possibility of middle and late life happiness.

This sense of desperation for a family has more to do with the mere biological insistence that we reproduce ourselves than with the fear of a lonely, unassisted second half of life. This fear is given usually as the reason, and is of course quite real, but is being forty, single and childless really the black pit many people assume it is? On the contrary, making it this far into life without becoming tied to a spouse or child or both, or having had the guts to leave a mediocre marriage at this point, may be

Part 2: Laying the Foundation for Lasting Happiness

cause to celebrate. Break down the situation into its real possibilities instead of viewing it as something vaguely to be dreaded.

What about the terrible loneliness? I say why should this person be lonely? Instead of having to be with someone every night, she or he might socialize only when they are really in the mood to socialize.

As to being less physically attractive at this age, I really don't see how that should harm their chances to find a partner, even if it were true. For as a person gets older they become more attractive not less—they become *deeply* attractive as opposed to youthful good looks which are *superficially* attractive. What's more, many of these older people not only possess subsurface attractiveness but they have more to say on more subjects with more conviction, wit, wisdom, and charm. And—voila!—it seems these days you can have it all: with medical advances successful pregnancies are becoming common for woman in their forties. And yet the question remains: how are you to control mating impulses until you're thirty or forty?

It certainly is not easy, and yet it is far from impossible. And with the knowledge that there are several major incentives for not yielding to the call to mate at once it should be easy to be creative in searching for an alternative outlet for these impulses. In addition to the ones given above, here are some more major incentives for postponing these big commitments:

> • You and your partner will most likely be more secure in your abilities, knowledge (both general and professional), career.

> • You will probably have not only more money coming in but also have amassed a respectable savings to fall back on in emergencies.

> • Even more importantly, you will have come to know yourself and other people and the opposite sex much better than ten years previously, and so be substantially equipped to judge who might be likely to contribute to your happiness and well-being

Happy Between Relationships

in the long term, instead of just knowing who physically attracts you.

- You will be less ruled by passion, less likely to be swayed by it when making major life choices, and yet still be capable of passion and even more so of love—a deep, steady, ever-expanding love.

Use mating impulses to achieve other goals. Like electric current, mating impulses can be diverted from a straight path by the creation of a network of equally or more conductive branches. But first what is needed, and what does a world of good at any time in life, is patience. Some measure of patience is needed to pursue any deliberate goal; whereas a lack of it inevitably achieves only primitive human Nature's goals: a spouse, a baby, a hand to mouth existence, and minimal shelter. Patience is available to anyone who can convince himself there is no need to rush. And not only is there no need to rush into a family, there is also no need to rush into trying to achieve other goals of any kind. Rushing is never productive of anything worthwhile. There is always more time than there seems, and it is best to work at something carefully and exhaustively over a prolonged period, including relationships, even though others might seem to be achieving their dreams quickly and easily—which is probably an illusion anyway.

Once patience, just a little patience, is added to the mix, then all that remains is to latch on to some exciting goals. And once sexual energy is bridled and set galloping in pursuit of non-fleshly objects, watch out. You may find yourself making outrageous progress where previously any progress had seemed like a miracle.

Sex is, after all, the major driving force in the world, so powerful that it is able to overcome, time and time again, that which never fails to bring down the mightiest among man and beast, Death. With the life force tightly focused on non-reproductive goals, you cannot help being happy, having transformed your project into your lover; and a very special lover at that, being one that not only fills your life with interest but—say your project is to start your own business—may well propel you to the fulfillment of professional dreams. So it is not a question of

Part 2: Laying the Foundation for Lasting *Happiness*

whether the pursuit and possession of career dreams is better or not as thrilling as sexual pursuit and possession—it *can be* sex, or at least love-making of the highest order; and without the remotest possibility of the appearance of any kind of sores as a result.

21.

Becoming Forever Young

When a person becomes an adult he or she soon has pressed upon her or him the real need for being mature and responsible. The first step for many people toward achieving these essentials of a successful adulthood is to remove the tendencies of teens and pre-teens. In other words they stop smiling, or smile only when it is discourtesy not to or when it is appropriate in various social settings. Playing becomes as unthinkable as assaulting the boss, while playful remarks and such are vented to let off stress among friends in mainly off-color form, which is acceptable being considered "adult."

Not that any of this makes becoming really responsible or mature any more likely to occur. In fact I think it is more likely to have the opposite effect. Being suddenly reduced to a picture of the rest of your life as serious business, where having fun is at best a pardonable vice and at worst a minor sin, real vices (adult ones of course) may be turned to for consolation.

It is my contention that the youthful signs of energy, high-spirits, and whimsicality are necessary—in a controlled degree—for the survival of these qualities. It is also my contention that these qualities are among the most useful in adult life—both professionally and personally. The Yiddish poet Abraham Sutzkever said "If you carry with you your childhood, you never become older." Without the survival of certain features of your childhood attitude and behavior, life can quickly lose much of its light and even its meaning. Without the survival of:

- insatiable curiosity
- high intensity

Part 2: Laying the Foundation for Lasting Happiness

- genuine friendliness
- vigorous motion
- love of play

And the closer you can come to these qualities universally, and the closer you can come to an art for art's sake manner—that is, for the sheer love of doing each thing regardless of the reward for doing it—the more you become that person who has it all: the adult child. The adult child has:

- fantasies he or she brings into reality;
- games which increase career knowledge and general wisdom;
- play sessions that are not limited to a locality but have the potential to extend literally over the whole world, as well as backward and forward in time.

What, on the other hand, does an ordinary adult do when the ordinary adult wants to display as much of his or her adult dignity (a word virtually synonymous with mature adulthood) as possible? Nothing, basically. Nothing, that is, but sit or stand as still and straight as possible, speaking as little as possible with as little animation of gesture or facial feature as possible, or perhaps stiffly reading a book.

This to me is false dignity, more like death than dignity. Everything that a child does or says is full of life, full of the true dignity. Of course, much of what children do is reckless, piddling, inefficient, and messy—though cute it must be said. However if you can look beyond these imperfections (which, appearing in serious adults, would shock certain other serious adults and be thought anything but cute), their motivations and reactions in these unbecoming situations are admirable.

When a child makes mud patties she or he is getting messy it's true, but the child is also showing curiosity, industriousness, and a oneness with nature. And there is no grinding quality about the curiosity or industriousness, nothing but excitement and laughter. When a child falls down and hurts a knee, he or she gives full expression to actual natural feelings instead of stifling pain and turning it inward, as adults

Happy Between Relationships

do with all forms of pain. A child will sometimes say 'Hi' to a complete stranger who is alone and ask personal questions. This is sometimes embarrassing to the parents. But the child is just being friendly, partly because she or he is once again curious, but probably even more so because he or she wants to be friendly and make the solitary stranger feel less alone. And they smile and wave when it's time to say goodbye.

The great English writer, lexicographer, and colorful character, Dr. Samuel Johnson wrote in a letter "Allow children to be happy in their own way, for what better way will they ever find?" Children have captured the most essential components for human happiness; adults let them escape or go into hibernation, partly through focusing on the negative details of each new complication that adulthood brings. But I feel that it is even more a kind of putting into cold storage anything at all they remember doing as a child or adolescent that causes this loss. Of course it's a good thing to rid yourself of all of the specific silly mistakes you made in these early stages of development; to behave in a shrewd adult way, throwing off childish helplessness and using to the full the wisdom you've gained from hard experience. And yet just because you made mistakes, and some may have been embarrassing then and now, look at the spirit that went into those mistakes!

What adults need to do is remain children at heart. This is shocking advice, I know. What could be more shameful than being a thirty-five year old child? But I don't think shame would result from being a thirty-five year old child; that is, if the child is a mature child. A little confusing? Let me explain. As I mentioned, children have captured the most essential components for happiness—one look at a group of them playing would convince anybody of this. However, because certain childish conditions of mind carried into adulthood (like being unacquainted with basic things such as good manners) are harmful to any kind of success, we think anything child-like must be put behind us. This is the greatest of tragedies. A case of literally throwing out the baby with the bath water. I know it's an oxymoron, a mature child, but what's wrong with a good oxymoron? And it gets to the heart of the matter.

Part 2: Laying the Foundation for Lasting Happiness

A mature child who is thirty-five is not a Peter Pan if male or a Helpless Helen if female. He or she is a child at heart, also a child at brain to a healthy degree, with an experienced and knowledgeable hunk of wise gray matter at the reins. The wise gray matter in the brain sees the healthy happy childlike parts of the brain not as mosquitoes plaguing important expeditions through its jungle; it sees them more as raw and rugged Jeeps, happy to go bouncing endlessly over rough and uncertain jungle roads in search of whatever the expedition scientists are after.

In other words preserving or rejuvenating the best of your childish behavior will benefit every aspect of your life. The boundless energy you will derive from the boundless curiosity and enthusiasm of a child makes wonderful discoveries and achievements possible. You are a hundred times more likely to achieve a higher level of success or find an exciting new activity if you attack the world with certain childlike qualities than grim adult determination. If you set out on a mission to improve your life, curiosity, humor, delight in the spectacle of activity, and so on, lead to perseverance, creative inspirations, a winning personality and on and on; while grim determination is soon worn down with the strain, and is not pleasant to look at or be around.

So, how can you get back these good qualities of children that you got rid of long ago? I think it boils down to a fundamental attitude toward what surrounds you. A child, as I mentioned, is curious about everything it encounters—no exceptions. If you as an adult can manage to make yourself look into, however briefly yet sharply, the things that pass through your environment, and simply note them for what they *actually* are, you have made a good start. This is because adults all too often assume what a thing is at a glance; or assume they have seen most everything before, so that if what is in front of them is not blatantly strange it's not worth two seconds of their time. There is always something around you which holds interest—even in a room with nothing new in it where you spend time every day.

Take ten seconds to look around you now—even if you're reading me in the bathroom. (If you are really in the bathroom, my book having become a bathroom book, I am not offended—at least it is being read.) Yes, let's suppose you are in the bathroom, even if you're not, to show

Happy Between Relationships

that curiosity might extend anywhere. Short of into the bowl itself, there are several places where overlooked details might create a spark of diversion. Look at the pattern on the Kleenex box, the design of the faucet and handles, the color and texture of the hand towels. How often do you notice them? Whether they spark little or no real interest or whether they strike you as decorative beauty, the simple fact that you are probably seeing their details consciously for the first time in months or years cannot help causing a stimulation like interest.

You might try working your way up from humble items like those mentioned above to things in your living room, your yard, the street with its traffic, pedestrian traffic, and so on. Then when you finally encounter familiar individuals you may actually see them, see something new in them, or see better how they see you. They may suddenly seem much less predictable and boring, more intriguing; and so may the masses of strangers whose normally blurred features are usually just so much human wallpaper.

There is an aspect of the child's typical attitude that is particularly useful to the person who is between relationships. It's the fact that children experience joy and happiness without sexual romance. Someone might say: "So what; that's only because they don't have the urges yet. They are only familiar with a narrow asexual world without all the possibilities of love romance and desire." This is true, but the fact remains that children do know joy and happiness in spite of this handicap. And I think it is safe to assume that if their joy and happiness is inferior to that experienced by adults deep in mutual romantic love, it is still enviable to unhappy adults. And it is questionable whether the giggling child is not actually happier than the love-drunk adult.

Someone else might say: "But how can you expect an adult to find things other than love and romance super-exciting: a child is seeing everything for the first time, so it's all fresh, all the kind of mind-blowing experience that love is for an adult." That may be so, but we needn't experience the same kind of joy or happiness as a child: wonder at all the basic shapes and motions of the world without understanding of basic purposes. And yet, with something like the curiosity and wonder of a child, adults can bring themselves to see the world from fresh

Part 2: Laying the Foundation for Lasting Happiness

aspects.

And, what is really exciting, when adults can actually see things again as mature children, they bring many layers of knowledge and experience to be applied to their observations. And enthusiasm plus knowledge equals a thinker; and not only a thinker but a positive thinker. That is where you find non-romantic joy as an adult: from the child-like contemplation of the world and people around you, knowing that they are worth the study and bound to reward you with information, possibly useful, at least interesting and entertaining.

More than just seeing things for the first time, a child is seeing *only* them, is seeing the objects of the world in a largely unselfconscious way. And the child loves everything he or she sees more because of seeing them in a kind of unity than because of being unacquainted with any painful or monotonous aspects they may possess. The philosopher Bertrand Russell wrote of "the life in the infinite," which for him consisted of "worship, acquiescence, and love." These emotions and their variations, such as wonder and curiosity, extended to all they see, make up the essence of the religious feelings natural and untaught in the child. So what we are talking about here is essentially a loving reverence for everything, which children intuitively feel to be spiritual and sacred. They feel this to a degree that puts everything on the same level of importance as themselves, that in a sense makes organized religion redundant to them. Their wholehearted unconscious devotion to the essence of religion gives them the deepest most spiritual happiness.

And so it is not so much that children are experiencing new things while the adult has seen and done it all before: more like children see the continuity or connectedness of all things and involve themselves in the playful worship and love of all things. Adults become sold on the idea that self is, if not the only thing that's important, at least far more so than anything else, and become constantly preoccupied with themselves. Love of all things remains, however, a living emotion for adults, only in concentrated form in the idea of a perfect mate or baby—that is, other parts of themselves.

If they do not have something like the perfect mate and no children

Happy Between Relationships

then they commonly have a sense that what they are doing is being done so as to keep themselves occupied and healthy until the right person has been found. If they have a mate they love but are separated by whatever daily necessity, they are waiting to love, worship and acquiesce until they meet the right person again at home. As in the song by Brian Adams, " Everything I do, I do it for you." This is to say for myself, so that I can live a spiritual inner life of love, worship and acquiescence.

The child also lives in a self-absorbed way, but of a different kind. Instead of requiring other people to turn on their switch and fill the world with the light of meaning, the child can embrace the sunbeams directly. He or she is greedy for the energy and warmth of the sun on her or his skin, wants to be richly stuffed and crammed with every sight smell taste sound and feeling available, is nothing but one big take take take and no give attitude. Children want it all—all being much less to do with the ownership of slick possessions and the approval of their peers than it is with adults, and nothing to do, of course, with a spouse and children. Their self-absorption is of a superior kind, in my opinion. It is essentially a kind of no-holds-barred intellectual curiosity, a pure pursuit of knowledge for knowledge's sake and art for art's sake.

Now there is nothing stopping grown up people from exercising intellectual curiosity. The newness of most things in their general aspects is admittedly not present as with the child, but many of the details are. The possibility of discovering interesting amusing astonishing new bits of information about things you know in one way, perhaps know to the point of weariness, is almost always present. The conscious pursuit of these new discoveries will provide a joy in finding very comparable to the joy of a child. And childlike happiness is nothing to be ashamed of, it is the opposite of immaturity: it is simply the by-product of intellectual growth.

Part 2: Laying the Foundation for Lasting *Happiness*

Youth is happy because it has the capacity to see beauty. Anyone who keeps the ability to see beauty never grows old.

—Franz Kafka, writer

The heads of strong old age are beautiful beyond all grace of youth.

—Robinson Jeffers, writer

22.

Determining at What Age it is Hardest to Find Happiness

Most people in the U.S. (and elsewhere) would probably say, if only given five seconds to reply to the question: "Who is in a better position to be happy, a person in their twenties or a person in their sixties?" "A person in their twenties, of course!" using about two of the five seconds to make their selection. Not a surprising choice in a country so youth-obsessed that wrinkle cream is a multimillion dollar industry. Not a surprising choice when you look around and see older people either crippled or crabby or both.

Even if they don't have certain things—say looks, talents, money, charm, a good education or job, loved ones or good friends—young people at least have or are likely to have ample time to improve and acquire these things. And they are almost guaranteed to have certain things universally held to be cool. People in their twenties almost always have good energy levels; a large capacity as well as interest in sex; and resilience, both physical and mental.

But what is really attractive to most is not the reality but the image of youth. A twentysomething person, it occurs to minds bombarded with images of youth worship since the first time they were placed as toddlers in front of a TV, has really "got it goin' on". The luxuriant hair, perfect muscle tone, unblemished skin, bright smiling eyes and teeth, low body fat, easy friendliness romance intelligence and laughter—this is what young adulthood is all about, right? So who are all those clearly not old people who have thin hair, flabby arms and chubby thighs, crooked coffee-stained teeth, and laughter-resistant mouths?

Part 2: Laying the Foundation for Lasting *Happiness*

Happiness, however, does not reside in appearances. Whether a young adult looks like he or she is happier than an older person is really irrelevant to the question of happiness. We all believe that there exist happy young adults and happy older adults. Well then the questions to be asked are:

> 1) What are the typical causes of happiness with both young and old?
>
> 2) Which set of causes is the more likely to bring a deep sustainable happiness?

Typical ability to live happily between relationships should be a major part of the reckoning, because, as this book exists to point out, it is a major part of every phase of life—young or old, married or single.

First let's examine the roots of the happiness of some older people. On the surface it may seem miraculous that any person in their sixties is happy, considering the restrictions I mentioned earlier: limited physical activity, susceptibility to various aches and pains, etc. And yet maybe after a closer look at their circumstances it won't be so surprising. The bottom line for the older adult is that she or he has survived. They have been put through all the fiery torments, acid tests, and Chinese water tortures nature and civilization could devise to defeat them—and emerged from it all victorious. They can say to themselves "I've lived a life, the rest is celebration!" In addition to the pleasure of knowing they are life-competent, they have a vast catalog of thrilling, peaceful, absorbing, fun, moments to sip like champagne when in reflective mood; because, thankfully, when we can struggle through troubles we can usually find joys. Family is not always available, and, though it is usually much enjoyed when there, it is not essential on a daily basis—been there, done that.

The roots of happiness for a younger person are of course typically very different. A happy young adult is usually somebody who, on the other hand, not only revels in the idea of family, but has family as the motivating force for most of their actions. They are highly conscious that they are accomplishing all the transitional steps from childhood to

Happy Between Relationships

adulthood on or before schedule. They are either seriously dating, engaged to, or already married to, the person they believe is Mr. or Mrs. Right. They are on their way professionally, moving steadily from rung to rung up the ladder of success. They are already doing research on where the highest rated school districts are, and inquiring while they're at it if there are any new subdivisions in the area. Because it won't be long before they are in a position to put a down payment on a house. And if the marriage and the first child are not unreasonably delayed, then everything is in place for lifelong happiness and all that is needed now is to follow through. All that is needed now is for each family member to get a passing grade in the simple matter of family duty—a thing the happy twenty-five year old can't imagine won't happen, and so he or she is happy.

How often, though, are twenty-five year old people right on schedule, having established themselves in a dreamed-of marriage and career? And, for the few that appear to have achieved their ideal family unit, basing their happiness on it—what are the odds that it will continue to function on all cylinders, ever kindling the day's happiness?

The sixty-five year old, however, seems to possess better odds of achieving a continual happiness. Here is the essence of what seems to be their happiness advantage. They have learned, usually through the school of hard knocks:

  • that family cannot be relied upon to provide a daily allotment of happiness;

  • that even if the family's relationships are of the best quality, and do manage to supply wonderful boosts to your happiness almost every day, you are still responsible for making 90% of the time enjoyable yourself;

  • that you are the only one who has the potential to be a dependable supplier of happiness.

I think the older person who is enjoying life to its fullest extent must

Part 2: Laying the Foundation for Lasting Happiness

possess a philosophy which may be boiled down to this paradox: "In order for me to give you the best of myself as often as possible, I must be as selfish as I can most of the time."

Being selfish in this sense merely means making an effort to serve yourself, keeping yourself entertained, stimulated, and happy with a consistent quality effort of creative planning. This is done, as alluded to above, not just for your own good—-though every bit as much for this reason—but for the benefit of your spouse, children, relatives and friends. Because the idea of living for another or others, though on the surface it smacks of noble self-sacrifice and poetic love, produces an ignoble life. In addition to making you a slave to another person—a slave in both thought and action, for when you are not doing things *for* them you are thinking *about* them—you soon turn from a cheerful obedient servant into a miserable obedient servant. And, with life already seeming desolate most of the time, inevitably, whether it's true or not, the person being lived for manages to create the impression that he or she does not appreciate the efforts of the other. It is not an arrangement built to last.

Of course many older people do not turn their valuable lessons from youth to the best advantage, and remain in a misery that is steadily deepened as the physical burdens of age increase. But undoubtedly there are many who prosper through those lessons. At the same time, there probably exist young people who are not subject to the typical mistakes of youth, though I myself have never met one. It would probably be more accurate to rephrase this statement as, "though I myself have never met *him* or *her*."

There is virtually no chance of escaping adolescence and young adulthood without committing a spectacular array of mistakes, both major and minor. It's a time of extremism. You either sow your wild oats—partying, drinking, being sexually reckless, moving your body at high speeds, and generally searching out danger; or you are a social washout—painfully shy. Both these types are capable of being highly intelligent, outstanding achievers; they are also both capable of ending up as miserable creatures if they don't learn to strike a balance and find moderation in life. Disenchanted with the paradises they imagined they

Happy Between Relationships

had found, say the party scene or the Internet, and which they had entirely relied on for happiness, they become hopeless and bitter. Even those who early strike the necessary balance between career, family, friends, etc. continue to make major mistakes. As I mentioned above, many of this group feel they have it made, with the rest of their lives bound to consist of nothing but family-based bliss.

So what exactly is it that the younger generations of adults might learn from the more well-adjusted of the older generations? I think most generally speaking this would be knowing yourself and the matter at hand as well as possible before making a major life-decision. Of course a younger person isn't likely to be able to acquire anything approaching a comprehensive understanding of such subjects as marriage, parenthood, relationships before they have to make serious decisions in these areas—these are very complex subjects! However, taking a cue from the knowledgeable and shrewd tendencies of wise and happy age, the less experienced person can at least know enough to steer clear of mistakes from which it takes years to recover, or from which you can never recover. And while it is true that most of these happily wise and wisely happy older people didn't get to be this way without making many mistakes in life, why shouldn't the newer generations make less?

All it takes is—what is hard for the young and cocky, as I know from personal experience—a willingness to admit that you haven't got it all figured out. This makes it possible to become a student of things like relationships, marriage, parenting—instead of blindly following some early-formed fairy-tale notions on these subjects, or, just as dangerous, viewing these subjects solely in terms of your own parents' behavior in these areas.

Becoming a student of things like relationships marriage and parenting is all about observation, unbiased analysis, and reading. If you take time now and then to look sharply around you, you will find an abundance of clues about the dynamics of relationships. But this is not so easy as it sounds.

Being sunk deeply in your own plans and problems is the norm for most people most of the time. They rarely see the details of other lives,

Part 2: Laying the Foundation for Lasting Happiness

distorted as they are like censored TV images by the thick filters of self-preoccupation. Even the people who are seen on a daily basis are subjected to this filtering of the telling details of their behavior, perhaps especially so as they are usually taken for granted. Often in the case of a long-running romantic relationship the filter is not turned off until the point when neglect of warning signs has allowed the bond to deteriorate beyond repair. On the other hand, intense early involvement in a romance often creates total blindness regarding everyone else, while at least bringing you out of self-absorption enough to focus on the person you're in love with. Often to the point of reading meaning in the meaningless—like a yawn or a blink. Life's little ironies!

Although it's quite possible to observe and analyze a variety of people's relationships well while in a relationship, when you are unattached is the ideal time. When you are unattached there is no direct pressure to come to conclusions on such issues as: who may or may not be a good match for marriage, how many (if any) kids you may want, the best ways to conduct relationships within a family, and so on. When someone is clearly waiting for you to make up your mind as to your feelings about the future of the relationship, it is very difficult to deliver an answer coming from mature thought based on solid observation and research. Emotions tend to dominate. And yet emotions, though frequently sweet and often noble, are not very smart and can and will land you underneath a load of misery. Study carefully the couples you see and read books on relationships. This is just another highly practical use for your time between relationships—one that could pay big dividends in terms of family or relationship harmony later on.

23.

Continuing to be Happy Between Relationships in Your Next Relationship (Or the Need for Passion in the Workplace too)

The simple fact is that we are all between relationships on any given day. No matter how well matched or how fresh their love, a couple cannot possibly bring a sense of interest and enjoyment to every waking hour of each other's day. It's physically and psychically impossible! Even on a honeymoon, where work and routine chores do not exist to keep them apart. No matter how well-suited the couple on this honeymoon are to keep each other entertained and how unnaturally continuous their efforts, the end result would fall well short of a verdict of totally blissful submersion in each other. At best it might be judged by them in an honest appraisal as 80 percent bliss 20 percent nauseating torture—a kind of cross between having eaten too much chocolate and a bee stuck in your ear.

In normal conditions, however, a near complete reversal of this smothering is commonplace in relationships. Work, with the havoc variable or different hours can and will play on your ability to get together, makes certain people spend more time alone than in their relationships. Can a good relationship carry over and make these hours apart happy? I don't say it's never happened, but I do say it's never lasted if it has. A thought here and there through the workday of a partner's lovable qualities, or what is planned for your time together later, may be sumptuous dining but it is not filling. By itself it is not enough to tide you over until the next installment of nourishing love. This would seem to imply that your work must be sufficiently interesting to make the time flow away at a tolerable speed—to provide, in other words, filling if not thrilling food until you can return to the real feast

Part 2: *Laying the Foundation for* Lasting *Happiness*

at home. But this won't cut it; it may fill, but it has no chance of *fulfilling*.

Work, either the kind you have to drive to and from or the kind which leads you to take classes or find and read a series of books, must always be a love. It needn't be a first love, but it had better be something you can feel some kind of, if not passion for, at least excitement about in some respect. And if your job is not inherently lovable you should try to find a way to make it so (read on for suggestions on how to do this) or find a way to get one you can. Why is work so crucial even when you're in a good relationship? Two reasons, one of them obvious, the other perhaps even more obvious—both of them given far less than their proper weight, their force being diverted to serve the all-consuming idea of love relationship.

The more obvious than obvious reason that you have to love your work is that you have to live it all day long. Even if you are a housewife (or househusband) living the part is far from easy, indeed hardly sustainable, when the only motive for doing the work is to support the relationship. On the other hand, with a love for the work itself, such as the challenge of raising a child well, or the freedom to get household chores done quickly and thus be able to set aside time for pursuits, being a housewife becomes easy and a joy. And so what I am saying is in essence the common sense that for the relationship to be healthy the people in it must preserve and promote their mental and physical health during the day—common sense.

The just plain obvious reason you have to love your work is yet often subtly twisted if a person is in or plans to be in a love relationship. Work becomes, above all else, overwhelmingly, sometimes solely, the financial engine of the relationship. The force of the relationship may become an effective factor in bringing advancement or acquiring the skills or degrees that make for hefty salaries, yet it does not care if you like it. The relationship you see is an animal and, like any animal, is only concerned with the fulfillment of its immediate survival needs, such as making sure it has enough to eat, etc. The only difference between your furry or feathery animal and that of a relationship being that the latter is hungry in *several* ways instead of just one.

Happy Between Relationships

The relationship-animal may be self-centered, but it has to be in order to survive. It must ensure the conditions exist in which it has the best chance of survival, meaning to its simple practical animal mentality four things—quality time in the relationship and money money money. The only problem here is that no matter how hard the people raising the animal try to convince themselves the gorgeous palomino or majestic lion is all that matters, they can't believe it except superficially. A persistent but polite and familiar voice (their own) regularly reminds at the animal's feeding time that he or she is going hungry.

An ideal way for the people raising the relationship animal to feed is through work. But the awareness that a healthy paycheck will be the result of this work is not health food. It is one of the ingredients of the health food of well-being to be sure, but by itself money is just cabbage—hardly a spiritual feast. Work is an opportunity for action as dynamic as any which a relationship is capable of sparking. It may be thought that this is only possible in a person's ideal job. Not necessarily so. With a full slate of dynamic elements ripe for exploitation in the majority of workplaces, it's usually the worker's fault if he or she doesn't have an impetus besides money to get working each day. What's so dynamic about a store, a maze of cubicles, a bank, or office? Here are the built-in dynamics all these situations have in common. Opportunities to:

- learn new skills;
- make innovations;
- master machinery;
- become more efficient in every area of life.

Opportunities to:

- be with and learn the inner workings of a group of people (coworkers);
- meet new people (customers) every day;
- impress them with your cleverness friendliness and general charm;
- be impressed by the cleverness friendliness and general charm

Part 2: Laying the Foundation for Lasting *Happiness*
of these new people.

The keynotes to all of these activities are creative self-expression and a passion for the study of people. The idea of studying people may seem pretentious, possibly evoking images of the gods on mount Olympus gazing down through the clouds at the follies of mankind. But I think of it as a form of self-analysis. The way you react to other people in every instance is a detailed self-report. To the honest self-analyst, a reaction on any scale to someone else's behavior is always a revelation on the state of your overall outlook, as well as an indication of passing moods. You can also make work interactions tend a lot more to your ease and advantage if you make an effort to understand people. But, aside from these egoistic considerations, here is a wonderful opportunity for people to provide each other with the very effort at understanding which translates to caring in deeper relationships.

And, speaking of caring in deeper relationships, there is no better way to show you care than by caring properly for yourself in these relationships.

24.

More on Building Independent Happiness in the Midst of a Relationship

※

One of the biggest pitfalls in life is the mistake of thinking that once we are established in a mutual love relationship set on a sound financial foundation bliss must ensue. This is far from the case. In fact the emptiness you feel when you discover that this alone raises the fuel tank indicator of your happiness only part way, is much deeper than the emptiness felt by those who are lost and lonely by themselves. They quickly come to realize that there still exist vast spaces of very unblissful moments in each day. And while it is true these are meagerly compensated for by the brief quality time together—this inevitably falls short from time to time of the desired quality.

The most common remedy for this horrible sensation of burning in paradise is to convince your partner that it's time to have children. When the child has been had it is found to be cute and a miracle but miserably inappropriate as a gap filler. Instead of imperfect bliss the couple is now faced with a nightmarish burden where there would have been joyful service if they had had the child for the right reason—the desire to give a child the benefit of their wisdom and love for life. And this is a very difficult benefit to give a child if you do not possess either one when the child is born. It's a very tough situation.

What is needed instead of a child, or rather to make the parents fit to raise a child, is not merely an interesting activity or pursuit not involving their spouse but an entire system of behaviors calculated to bring *independent* happiness. It should be so complete and so solid a structure that any damaging changes to the relationship that may come about over time will not bring the building down; whereas if the love continues

Part 2: Laying the Foundation for Lasting Happiness

and grows stronger you may achieve something of a Sistine Chapel before the end. In other words your luck in having found love must be viewed and treated as a *bonus*, a special turbo charged bonus it is true, and yet hardly more capable of bringing happiness by itself than a turbo charged sports car.

One of the reasons for this is that, even when love persists over many years, it is still a changeable thing, subject in every case to wide swings in intensity and the taking on of new guises, not always pleasing. But perhaps a more important reason for not basing happiness on your love is that you cannot be involved in the activities of love or even the thoughts of love day and night. In fact even in the most passionate days of the relationship there are still a good number of hours not being filled with love as the primary ingredient—you need to have a *diversity* of interests to give each hour of your life at least the *potential* to be interesting. If you live for love then you are dying most of the time.

A system for developing independent happiness might consist of such general ingredients as the following. First must necessarily come the openness of mind to look beyond the family for fulfillment, realizing that it is not un-American to do so, especially as finding a life outside the marriage will only strengthen such things as 'family values'. Possessed with an open outlook, the next step is to determine what would be likely candidates for complementing your marriage *and* job. Because even with satisfying careers it is still essential to find numerous other interests on your own; because, though a career usually means a lot of time away from your spouse, it is still an intimate component of the marriage, providing its material life blood. Other independent activities should have reference to only yourself, contributing to the marriage significantly in the long run but only indirectly through a more stable sense of well-being.

(By the way, if one of the partners in the marriage is not working they might consider planning or returning to a career. If they are both working, but one at a career the other at a job, then the latter might decide to pursue a career as a substantial independent activity; and the one with the career might consider and research alternative careers so as not to feel helplessly chained to one profession.)

Happy Between Relationships

Candidates for cleanly independent activities might include some of the following:

> • Going on wandering drives alone to think without interruptions, listen to music, explore your area, and to really take in the scenes of a day or evening, which is less effectively done with the distractions of a passenger or an appointment.
>
> • Joining social clubs, ones you have never belonged to before, to make fresh acquaintances with people who do not (and may never) know your spouse or anything about your marriage.
>
> • Finding new outdoor retreats with no associations with your past or any person. Preferably in a beautiful natural setting, where you can go to escape all people and reminders of people and let nature's voice get through to instruct and soothe.
>
> • Finding new restaurants of a kind you do not usually go to, in order to have a quiet or lively place to go for a completely different set of distractions than usual. Here you might read without the interruption of conversation, or just take the time to savor unusual food while doing some leisurely people-watching.

One of the greatest joys of establishing a routine of independent pleasures is that the routine may be changed on a whim or returned to on a whim. The marriage state is at the opposite pole. Meals, evening activities, such as which television shows are watched and which movies are rented, going out for dinner, going on vacation, being romantic, making love—everything is contingent on at least some measure of agreement on your partner's part. And if a marriage can be a democracy it will also be a bureaucracy at times. Change of routine is possible, but usually requires efforts resembling those needed to overcome bureaucratic red tape, with the added drawback of having to live with the pouting bureaucracy afterwards. The same is true of friendships, though to a lesser degree.

Part 2: Laying the Foundation for Lasting *Happiness*

So you see one of the major benefits of independent happiness: it gives a relationship the balance it badly needs.

25.

What is *Real* Happiness?

※

Qualifying as a happy person is really a fairly simple feat to achieve if you're a resourceful optimist. You can start at the top of the list of conventional blessings with items like 'wonderful spouse and beautiful kids' and calmly work all the way down. "Well maybe we fight all the time and the kids take drugs, but at least we're together—that proves we're basically happy." Or " Well, I'm divorced and the kids have dropped out, but at least I have a house and a good job—I'm happy because since I'm finally rid of those head cases I have room to breathe and relax." Or "So I've lost my job because of my drinking and had to sell the house and move into a tiny apartment, anyway I'm still in my early forties with much life still ahead—I'm happy because there's nowhere to go but up and plenty of time to get back on my feet." Or "So I'm in jail for killing a child while DUI, so what—I'm happy just to be alive!" I'm convinced that for some people a bare-bones happiness can be constructed out of every conceivable circumstance except one: death. Actually death should be the ultimate bare-bones experience, shouldn't it?

Of course there are also people who build a fully fleshed misery out of a wide range of circumstances, plus death—death calmly playing a starring role. But a non-bogus happiness is a richer experience than the optimistic sort; it is richer and therefore more complex. It consists of a harmony and a balance between the various elements that make up your day, and a harmony and a balance between what you do and what you think. Let's explore this harmony and balance.

Real happiness is like a vigorous piece of music—like a powerful classical composition. Often the most memorable and meaningful works

Part 2: Laying the Foundation for Lasting Happiness

are composed of several distinct moods and alternating intensities—alternating usually between high and high, just in a different form. For example, in many works by Beethoven there are passages where a difficult and complex struggle at a slow, deliberate tempo gives way to a helter-skelter flood of joyful strains at overcoming this difficulty. There are rich repetitive melodies which build or shift, and which are overlaid with interweaving outgrowths of the original, causing the whole to flower in unanticipated colors and forms.

This is what happiness must consist of if it's to qualify as real: not just one cool melody, hip rhythm, or infectious groove surrounded by various kinds of empty droning; cool hip and infectious rhythms melodies and beats being ever developed to be simpler now, now more complex, always under construction or deconstruction, never reduced to a dead-air drone. Real happiness means that your music is always calling you and always within reach. Real happiness means that your frustration level is high—but only because you can't find enough time in twenty-four hours to make half the music that comes into your head.

The grand thing about this kind of real happiness (not ideal happiness, which means a fairy-tale conception of happiness that wouldn't satisfy if it were possible) is that money and job type have nothing to do with it. Education is not required either, as long as the desire to learn is present and capable of being applied. What is totally essential, however, is that passions, other than just people you are passionate about, be thought about dreamed about and pursued! Because loved ones are to be loved but, however deeply you and they are capable of loving and being lovable, they just can't be allowed to monopolize all the love. Two very practical reasons exist for this:

> 1) the fact that love has been known to cool die or be removed, and

> 2) the equally hard fact that loved ones can't usually be in continual contact day and night.

For real happiness, you must spread love out over the whole day, so that each hour is brightened by the smiling appearance, though it may

Happy Between Relationships

be brief, of one of your lovers. Lovers!? No, not that kind of lover. The lovers that you must rendezvous with to supplement your love life are stimulators of your mind not your erogenous zones. I call them lovers because, if used passionately, they can do your soul good in the same way good love does. And in spite of their braininess they can be highly attractive, fun-loving, witty; best of all, these loved ones never heard of divorce or even separation—and they are immune to AIDS and STD's. What I am talking about is your imagination; the more challenging aspects of your work; the book you carry with you everywhere; the clever remarks you think of to say to coworkers. Look for many more potential lovers throughout this book; also look for them in places of your life I don't mention—-they lurk everywhere, just waiting to entertain and fulfill.

Imagine:

- a lover or loved one at your beck and call night and day;
- a new one for every new mood;
- and all of them either a good fit for that mood or easily discarded and replaced by a good fit.

Why not view all the ways you can think of to activate the higher abilities of your brain in a romantic manner? A book that enthralls you or a project that challenges you can do to your mind what a sexual lover can do to your body—and the pleasures last a lot longer. All it takes, just as in Peter Pan, is the realization and the belief that you can fly this way. Viewed this way, these commonplace things take on the urgency the desirability—all the driving forces previously controlled mainly by the genitals and the stomach. Real happiness in fact might well be defined as a continual feeling of being surrounded by desirable objects, all within reach, which tug at you with magnetic urgency.

And of course the single life is full of opportunities of surrounding yourself with desirable objects. This is how I myself see the single life: as a time of fullness, of nonstop sowing growing and harvesting. A time of busyness and bounty. In the next Part I will detail the causes of this more than optimism and show how the single life can be made not

Part 2: Laying the Foundation for Lasting *Happiness*
just tolerable but a good thing.

Part 3

Making the Single Life a Good Thing

※

Part 3: Making the Single Life a Good Thing

26.

Exterminating Loneliness and Boredom

Loneliness and boredom need not—should not—exist. Not only should they not dominate anybody's life, they should be totally exterminated—like cockroaches. None should be allowed to linger and breed. They are obsolete notions, born of the old world's aristocracy's ability to live the high life without working. Instead of using their golden opportunity to *do* things, many chose simply to sink into their social environment. Their happiness consequently became based on their relationships; when they were alone they felt lonely and bored, and with reason—they had no other interest in life, nothing even to fill the time. Some, under the influence of loneliness and boredom, wrote poems about desperate lovers.

On the other side of the coin there were the laborers, who worked virtually every hour they were awake. Did they feel loneliness and boredom? No not these same emotions; though perhaps a remote weak echo of them, if anything could be felt through the numbing fatigue. When alone, their minds cried for sleep, not for lovers or romance.

Today we have a little better balance between the rich and the poor—not in the disparity of incomes, but in the work done for those incomes. Both groups—plus the new middle class—work hard for their money, and all have at least a few hours each day at their own disposal. They also have entire days off each week, and most have vacations each year. The result, for some reason, is that everybody plays the idle aristocrat of old whenever they have free time—doing as little as possible, feeling more or less lonely and bored, sometimes even in company, especially when it is made up of a person or persons seen daily. Watching TV, surfing the Web, seeing a movie—these excellent

Part 3: Making the Single Life a Good Thing

means of entertainment and information are all too often misused by all classes as nothing but idle expressions of loneliness and boredom.

Now, how to make it practical for today's workers to do something with their precious free time? How can they, why should they, at the end of a hard day or week, make the time more than just relaxing? Isn't that enough? I answer that it isn't enough, because relaxing, by itself, is boring and takes you nowhere and, especially for singles, it leaves that lonely incomplete feeling. I can give the solution in one line; but let me preface it by saying this is the entire solution to the problem of boredom: at work, at home, anywhere. Here it is: work while you play and play while you work. This means simply the following:

> • That both you and your work can benefit from a light-hearted attitude and an alert sense of humor, because this makes you relax and have fun—a much more energetic and fertile state of mind than that of being stressed and grave.

> • That you can go from the 'comfortably numb' technique of rejuvenating yourself in your free time to one that works much better and allows you to make yourself wiser and stronger at the same time—what I call self-productivity.

And while the extermination of boredom and loneliness does not by itself result in real happiness, it is a giant leap in that direction.

27.

Exploding the Notion that Boredom is Part of Life

One of the most absurd things in the world is boredom. Under no circumstances whatsoever is there reason or excuse for it. Because, no matter what you may think now, you have not:

- seen everything worth seeing;
- done everything worth doing.

Nor do you:

- know everything worth knowing.

Moreover, you have:

- only seen a *small fraction* of what is worth seeing;
- only done a *small fraction* of what is worth doing.

With the throwing off of self-pity and a small effort of creativity, boredom can be crushed and crushed *easily*. (Use the techniques presented in this book as a starting point and foundation for this creativity.) Boredom is really nothing other than peevishness. Or wallowing in a lazy apathy. And if there is no excuse for boredom then apathy is downright unpardonable. People just don't realize, or if they do they don't feel it in their gut I have to believe, how fortunate they are to have an opportunity for living. I was the same way myself until I experienced first hand the death of someone just beginning to live who also happened to be dear to me. That was enough to make me *feel* how unpardonable apathetic people really are.

Part 3: Making the Single Life a Good Thing

There are a few general keys to forgetting that the concept of boredom was ever known to you. The first and foremost is the desire to shun forever the meager pleasures of feeling sorry for yourself because you are so bored. All it takes is to know and believe that wherever you are, whoever you are, whatever you're doing, there are rich resources available for giving you a far greater, and far more constructive, pleasure. Generally these resources may be termed:

1) Artistic thinking.

2) Artistic observation.

They should be constantly employed whether you are in a physically limited situation such as the workplace, or whether your time is your own and a range of activities are open to you.

Let me give you an example of artistic observing. (There will be much more later on artistic thinking and observation in Parts 4 and 5.)

When in a crowded place such as a mall or a restaurant try to identify what you would normally begin doing in automatic fashion when presented with a given set of circumstances. Say you are about to get into a line for a food court restaurant. Instead of looking upon this moment as quite a commonplace one, a real yawner, find something in your surroundings which interests you. And there's plenty of action, if action is a must for you to be interested in something. It's just subtle or something you think you've seen a million times. Take the guy working at the grill: not exactly a fascination for most people. But he doesn't have to be fascinating; interesting is all we're after in this situation. And he *is* interesting; *any* person doing just about anything is an interesting study. This is for two reasons: people are highly individual creatures who have unique reactions, if only slightly, to given situations; and, being of the same species, we are able, if we use concentration, to get some insight into the uniqueness of their personality as well as their current feelings. This is always at least amusing and diverting, sometimes downright enthralling.

28.

When am I Officially Between Relationships?

※

You can be between relationships in a larger sense and a smaller sense. Both can be the source of:

- bewilderment
- vague uneasiness
- emptiness
- panic
- out-of-your-head boredom
- excitement
- absorbing challenges
- sheer joy
- serene happiness

  The more obvious and larger sense—because of the much longer periods of time you are challenged to fill well—is that of simply being without a romantic partner. The smaller sense is more subtle, and calls for a set of definitions before it can begin to be addressed in an improving way.

The sense in which you can be between relationships in a smaller subtler—but no less distressing—way is this: by being left to your own devices *within* a romantic relationship. But the question here is: when am I officially between relationships? Because it's not just when you are separated by six jet hours and a three-day business trip that you need to be able to enjoy this world by yourself. (In the case of lovers separated by a business trip, by the way, someone might say that a dreary period of aloneness makes the reunion more exciting. "Absence makes the heart grow fonder," says the proverb. This may be so, but I

Part 3: Making the Single Life a Good Thing

strongly disagree about it requiring the lovers to be miserable or at any time even bored for this increase of fondness to be brought about. If the couple really enjoy each other's company to begin with, they cannot help becoming excited with the prospect of having many new things to talk about—and the more interesting things they have done in the period of separation the more they will have to discuss.)

There are many briefer, less dramatic, downright everyday, ways that a couple can and will be separated. Sometimes, in fact often, lovers are in effect separated when in the same room, even when their love for each other is still at the boiling point. If you think back on previous relationships, it is quite likely that there was even a time when you felt a sense of detachment from a lover while in the very act of love. Yes, between relationships with not a millimeter separating you physically! Then of course there are the plain workaday separations that occur each day like clockwork: during sleep, on the job, in the bathroom, and so on.

As for this last kind of separation—the daily inevitable kind—-though new lovers and love-idealists generally wish it were possible to spend every waking moment with their loved one, they would regret it if a good fairy granted their wish. Perhaps the more hard-core love-idealists would be able to continue to savor working as a team in a career as well as in raising a family. Perhaps they would be able to savor in a lasting way a partner's consistent willingness to sleep locked in an embrace; or maybe even to participate in mutual dreams, if technology ever makes that possible. However, I simply can't imagine that anybody in the world could stand to have constant togetherness in the bathroom. And I feel that there are many sincere though less hardy lovers out there who would fairly quickly start to feel suffocated by the constant presence of their partner in the other two areas as well. Most people have a need to be by themselves or with other people from time to time.

The problem is that the golden silence of being finally alone turns quickly to lead and the tedious wait begins to return to the other's arms and all the potential fun of togetherness. But without enjoying the time between togetherness, when you finally return to the beloved's side it

Happy Between Relationships

becomes a touchy balance and a catastrophe when upset. This is so because of the pressure of demands which must necessarily be placed on the relationship to churn a daily dose of concentrated happiness. And so any failure to deliver happiness, which could even happen without a lapse of attention to a partner's needs from sheer monotony, is sure to bring an emotional crash—or, what's even worse, a scaling down of your definition of happiness. This settling for a lukewarm happiness in a relationship is really just unhappiness putting on a happy face. When it comes to happiness there is never cause to settle; you can find the real thing. But how do you know when you need to provide your own happiness?

I think you should always provide your own happiness, not have it supplied to you. Even when in the middle of an animated conversation with someone you love, the only way to find it satisfying is to be at least an equal supplier of dialog. If you just sit there and wait for your partner to entertain you, you may be entertained but, like indiscriminately watching television, it is a passive kind of activity, like being whitewashed with happiness instead of becoming an artist and painting a happiness masterpiece. The key element in providing your own happiness is always *leaving a personal mark*. It's true that when you are together with the one you love many times you are given gifts of fun and pleasure that have little to do with your current behavior. These are a bonus, one of the perks of being in love, they should not be relied on to provide the staple of your happiness.

This being said, that you must provide your own happiness even with your partner, it makes sense to strive for happiness when separated by physical space or psychological distance from your partner. This returns us to the question of what constitutes being between relationships within a relationship? Because at these times you need to cue your inner resources to begin rolling at full force, and not expect someone else to provide a signal and a share of the impetus. When you are alone for any time at all you are between relationships, even if only for the time it takes for your partner to return from the kitchen or bathroom. Any time you are with your partner but not connecting mentally in a substantial way, you are between relationships.

Part 3: Making the Single Life a Good Thing

If you are sitting together on a sofa, for instance, bathed in the warmth of the other's presence, but not involved in conversation or romance, you need to act independently. Though perhaps watching television together, you are both in effect alone, immersed in thoughts that are unrelated except superficially by the action of the program. Your real interaction is with the program, so that if it is not something you find interesting, if it is something you agreed to watch because the other likes it, you might as well be in a vacuum. There's a warm loved presence, but it's little more than a warm loved ghost at the moment.

In the case of the various-sized blocks of time spent out of the presence of a romantic partner, there should be willing detachment. But not only should there be a willingness to be detached, there should be a willingness to forget the other person as far as possible. A willingness to lead a completely separate mental life, just as vital and thrilling as the one that revels in being in love. I say willingness because it is of course impossible when you are really in love not to think of the loved one from time to time when apart. But why stay obsessively on the theme of this person? It doesn't increase love, it often gives rise to suspicions.

When people are away from their romantic partner it may be a good idea to think of themselves as outside of their relationship, as having stepped out of one outfit and into another. And the new outfit, if worn with the right attitude, will resemble the uniform of the person happily not involved in a love affair. This attitude does not undervalue love; it merely reminds you of the importance (as well as the pleasure) of being a stand-alone individual, not incapable of functioning outside a social system. If you forget you are merely plugged in to the system (your love affair, marriage), being severed from it can feel like death. And, painful as it is to acknowledge this when in love, it must be remembered that chances are you will be on your own at some point before you die; you may as well prepare yourself to live happily then as well as now. On the other hand, when the object of love is present the independent lone-wolf attitude can be shut off like a light switch and the in-love switch can be thrown—with a resulting flood of interest and affection in the other, a surge of energy which, unlike the light bulb, is not followed by a burnout and can be renewed over and over.

Happy Between Relationships

"Let there be spaces in your togetherness" wrote Kahlil Gibran. This seems to me to be excellent advice to couples, both when they are separated by larger distances and virtually not separated by any physical distance at all. Where the couple are separated by no more than the distance of a sofa cushion, I think it is healthy to look on periods of psychological separation as not only inevitable but necessary. If pressure is felt by one or both of the partners to maintain a constant stream of communication, either verbal visual tactile, a tension is set up between them which quickly becomes tiring. If, through lack of much to say or shyness to open up, long stretches of disconnection become the norm, it is easy to become resolved to a lot of warm but empty isolation. There is no need to accept either condition.

In both instances asserting a need to fulfill independent desires while happily in the other's presence will create the necessary balance. This may mean doing a few simple chores like addressing envelopes or taking a few minutes to put away laundry, or it may mean reading a book or newspaper or writing a letter. If the other considers this a personal affront and the ruin of your quality time together, suggest a thing or two he or she might enjoy doing between occasions for more meaningful exchanges. If he or she wants no part of your scheme and insists you pay or pretend to pay continual attention to your togetherness, you might insist back or just do it anyway. If the other insists on being an unrelenting tyrant on this point, you may want to consider whether you want to be with an unrelenting tyrant. It is never healthy to let your independent self go unexpressed for any length of time; and luckily it almost always has the effect on your partner of granting a fresh-air breathing space.

And so being in a relationship is really made up of mostly a lot of being between relationships; or rather it should be for the success—which means the happiness—of the relationship. And the happiness of the relationship can be no greater than the happiness of each partner with their lives in total. The relationship itself, no matter how good, is incapable of supplying this—is in fact an unstable foundation on which to build happiness. The relationship itself is, if a good match, a bonus, a kind of whipped cream and cherry on a pie which has been filled with rich independent contents. You could almost look on a good relationship

Part 3: Making the Single Life a Good Thing

as not being in any way distinguished from the rest of your activities. It could almost be viewed as just another exciting activity on the list of things that make life worth living when not in a relationship at all. However, like the whipped cream or the frosting on the cake, the good relationship is a sugary spectacle, sweetening the whole—to cloying, if laid on too thick—while providing unique decoration.

Relationships, then, are a different species from the various closely related animals which make up your enjoyment of life when on your own. The complexity of happiness in a relationship becomes apparent when you consider that you must feed your own menagerie as well as help design, build, and then feed the animal of the relationship. With too much nourishment in one part of the zoo and not enough in another, the cries of starvation in one part would soon begin ruining digestion in the other part—if it hadn't already been ruined by overfeeding. In other words, being happy in a relationship is a complex balancing act. A relationship is worth pursuing with the right person; however if you neglect what you are independent of the relationship you are building without a foundation.

There is no easy solution to this difficulty of succeeding in a relationship. However, I think that being happy going into a relationship is the best possible start. Then you will have a variety of activities, which you will not let a bright new relationship fade, providing the "spaces between you". Thus being happy without a relationship will help a relationship with potential blossom. The trick is finding a partner who is also happy on their own.

29.

Putting the Time Between Relationships into Perspective

What is the best general attitude to take toward being between relationships? I will try to provide an answer to that question shortly, focussing in this Chapter on the person not in a relationship. First I want to give another definition of what may legitimately be considered the state of being between relationships. This is, again, to my mind a definition with multiple senses. There's the obvious one: the period from when a marriage or serious perhaps live-in romance ends to when you get involved in another one. Then there is the other more subtle condition, which is yet more widespread—in fact it is universal and occurs on a daily basis for everybody. I am talking about the times each day when you are by yourself. These add up to a large percentage of the day even in the closest relationships, and I believe that, even in the best possible situation, you must know how to enjoy these intervals to have real happiness.

Regarding those in relationships, even people who are married and have a strong realistic confidence that the marriage should not and will not end in divorce should prepare themselves to live happily alone. There is a simple reason why: people rarely die at the same time. And the best way of preparing for this natural fact is this: learning to rely completely on yourself for happiness.

This is not a cold-blooded way of looking at love; it is merely dealing with the negative possibilities and undoubted facts of love relationships in a sane way, so that when something happens that you don't want to happen it doesn't put you through unending hell. But besides that, to know that the foundation of our happiness is generated by independent

Part 3: Making the Single Life a Good Thing

thoughts and actions does not take away from love. It really has the opposite effect. For then the pressure is off the marriage or other serious relationship to continuously churn out the happiness. Love is freed up to take the role it is best suited for: being the desert of life, a fabulous dreamy desert with whipped cream and a cherry on top.

When you find yourself between relationships in the sense of being without a regular partner what, then, should be your general attitude toward the situation? Should it always be the same? That is, when getting a divorce or being divorced, when breaking up with a boyfriend or girlfriend on good terms or dumping or being dumped, when a spouse suddenly dies or dies after a long illness—can and should your feelings toward the loss and your new life be in any way similar?

Regarding the time it takes to pull out of the phase of reactive depression unavoidable in these situations, there is substantial variance among these cases. In the extreme case of the sudden death of a loved one, it might take two years even with the best outlook to feel intense happiness again. On the other hand, in the case of finally deciding to get out of an unhealthy relationship, with an exciting plan for living your new life, perhaps only a few days—or maybe even one night—should be enough to put that out of your way. (I got over the end of a year-old relationship myself in one night.) However, as wildly different as all of these traumatic experiences are, there is no reason for one to be any less excited than another about her or his new chances, as soon as they can bring themselves to consider them, of exploring new people and new life-styles. In this respect all breakups are the same: they are an opportunity to inject dramatic forms of freshness and newness into your life—let them be an air freshener instead of a means of suffocation.

One method of keeping a well-balanced perspective on your time out of a relationship is to remind yourself that one state is not necessarily superior to the other:

> • In one state you get intimate with another person, in the other you get intimate with your own mind.

> • In one state you make love, in the other you expand your

Happy Between Relationships

definition of love.

- In one state you enjoy being immersed in a single live personality, in the other you enjoy being immersed in a series of personalities, some live, some recorded.

For instance, you can be thrilled about the career and self improvements you've actually started since your break up, while at the same time think about how you might do things differently in your next relationship and look forward to doing them. Such as making sure you are happy between relationships within your relationship.

This essentially means that you are responsible for your own happiness every day. You must derive contentment, satisfaction, and peace from your own habits of thought and daily attention to projects dictated by well thought-out goals. But though goals and work should be fun, made fun if need be; though work should be stimulating in one way or another and goals should feel like warm living things, a life that is all goals and work is slavery and not sufficient to bring contentment, satisfaction, or peace. In order for you to reap the rich harvest of happiness to be had through positive thinking, working toward exciting attainable goals, and so on, you must add a little sparkle—in other words get even happier. This can be achieved readily through relationships with other people.

But this does not have to be a love relationship of any kind. Participating in relationships with friends, whether close or just acquaintances, parents, brothers and sisters, cousins (even remote ones), characters in books, television personalities, movie stars—even the most impersonal of these relationships can provide that spark of human contact which is an ancient need and joy for each of us without exception. So what we have is a formula where lone activities provide the basis of happiness, which is sparked into life and effect by a variety of relationships with other human beings.

In Parts 4 and 5 I will show how even these human contacts can be used in work while being enjoyed—the ultimate work, that of turning your life into art.

Part 3: Making the Single Life a Good Thing

Nothing is to me more distasteful than that entire complacency and satisfaction which beam in the countenances of a new-married couple.

—Charles Lamb, writer

Don't tell me marriage is still a safe haven any place in America. Well, maybe among the Amish.

—Herbert Gold, writer

30.

Overview of Marriage

※

According to a 1988 Gallup national survey, two out of three thirty-five to fifty-four-year-olds had divorced, separated, or been close to separation. And the fact is that approximately 50 percent of U.S. marriages are destined to end in divorce. Not to mention that of those who remain married many will do so only because the alternative looks even bleaker. Well, pretty depressing wouldn't you say? And yet, though most people have an inkling that something like the above statistics prevail, that all-pervasive license to do anything you feel an impulse to do is in place here as well: "It won't happen to me!" New criminals believe other criminals get caught, mountain climbers believe other climbers fall or freeze, jet passengers think plane crashes are something you see on the TV news and read about in the papers. Newlyweds, though far likelier to have their illusions smashed than frequent flyers or climbing enthusiasts, almost without exception believe that by saying the vows they have wrapped up a core of happiness to last a lifetime.

And yet a 'core of happiness' is precisely what is achieved by the lucky 25 or 30 percent of couples who manage to make love last. However, I wonder how much of the success of this group is really due to luck? Probably a substantial amount of it. Nevertheless it must be assumed that the right attitude during the process of choosing a mate goes a long way toward harnessing the services of luck. This attitude may well consist in:

- the desire to know someone thoroughly;

- to know yourself and what kind of person you are most likely to live in harmony with;

Part 3: Making the Single Life a Good Thing

- the patience to put off the big decision until at least one and a half of the first two items of this equation have been achieved.

The 'half' of course referring to self knowledge, which to gain a fully detailed picture of requires at least the better part of a lifetime; whereas the best one can hope for in the way of thorough knowledge of a partner before commitment is a fairly comprehensive but general idea of habits and tendencies.

And so how is one to get the healthy amount of patience needed to become confident in assessing yourself and others? The first step is to learn to become comfortable, contented, and even happy when you find yourself without a relationship. When this ability has been acquired it will be highly unlikely that you would ever settle for a clear mismatch through loneliness. And any periods of independence will allow for valuable stretches of solitude, which is the butterfly transformation from the caterpillar of loneliness, perfect for thinking studying and generally seeing things better. This will inevitably lead to better self knowledge; and this and the additional happiness, creativity and success it always brings, whether it results in finding a good marriage partner or not, is the purpose of this book.

While you're in this thoughtful unattached state it might be a good idea to consider what exactly marriage consists of. Whether you've never been married or are divorced, going over this ground will bring home the importance of making the right choice in a partner.

Detailing marriage routines

Everything in a marriage, both the good and the bad, consists of routines. Non-routine events in marriage, as in your life at every point regardless of the people in it or not in it, do not really influence a person's estimation of the overall quality of their existence. Finding a hundred dollar bill; winning at bingo; having an interesting conversation with a stranger by chance in a bookstore: all great, but fluky, nothing remotely to be depended upon to support happiness. But routine, on the other hand, though most of the word's connotations are negative, can be the foundation of your whole happiness as well as your unhappiness.

Happy Between Relationships

I list a brief series of marriage routines. Just dealing with the free-form period before the major complications of a child enter into the reckoning, there inevitably come into existence such routine items as: breakfasts and dinners (lunch possibly affording some creative leeway); conversation patterns; home eating habits; styles of arguing and making up; lovemaking tendencies; adjustments to other's delicate moods; adjusting to patterns of sleeping, sniffing, coughing, sneezing, clearing the throat, blinking, licking the lips, changing the clothes, washing the hands, brushing the hair and teeth, waking up, going to bed, clipping the nails—and every other personal item of business that you never would have become aware of if you hadn't married that person, but that it is impossible not to know in exact detail after no more than a week of wedlock.

Part 3: Making the Single Life a Good Thing

The trouble with many married people is that they are trying to get more out of marriage than there is in it.

—Elbert Hubbard, writer

Marriage is not just spiritual communion and passionate embraces; marriage is also three-meals-a-day and remembering to carry out the trash.

—Joyce Brothers, psychologist

Successful marriage is an art that can only be learned with difficulty. But it gives pride and satisfaction, like any other expertness that is hard won

—Benjamin Spock, psychologist

31.

Traditional Views

One good way to go about establishing your own unique formula for happiness is to question traditional views on happiness. Question whether they are:

- what you want now;
- what you want ever.

And this means everything that most everybody takes for granted as constituting a puzzle piece of that summer scene—including those enormous chunks of landscape: marriage and kids. Once this is done, with whatever results, these institutions are reduced to mere options on a level with any other of life's decisions: you can take it or leave it. The key is to look unflinchingly at every side of a thing; to bring to bear all of your resources of experience and analysis, without allowing fairy-tale cloudiness to float you into the center of the harsher realities of an ill-planned life. Let's briefly analyze some of the aforementioned institutions.

Let's start with the holy of holies. Marriage and kids. Why do people want them? Probably not because of what they observed of their own parents' experience while growing up. If anything that should sour a child on becoming a parent. Because, even if there are many happy memories, inevitably there are also horrifying pictures of parents as stress-monsters. And it's logical that the child would form some cause and effect ideas about their position as parent-spouse and their ugly behavior. So it would seem that their desire for this state springs from another stimulus. From a dreamy romantic haze? Something picked up from watching old Hollywood movies? Is it pure reproductive instinct?

Part 3: Making the Single Life a Good Thing

Fear of growing old alone? Boredom? Optimism in the face of abundant contrary evidence? The good outweighing the bad in their parents marriage and child rearing experiences? Yes, quite possibly every one of those reasons.

And they are all pretty good reasons. Because marriage and children are, all in all, quite nice really, given favorable circumstances. And yet why not face the bad? Why not look steadily into the eyes of the beast and determine whether its essence renders it a beautiful beast or a hideous one in your eyes? For it is my belief that, even given favorable circumstances, marriage and kids is not the best possible state for everyone. Or maybe it's not right for certain people at certain ages but excellent at other, later or earlier, ages. Thus a determining where you stand on the unavoidable routines etc., and a grasp of the feelings you are likely to experience in the midst of these routines, is essential to a chance of success.

32.

That Ring of Permanence

There is a ring of permanence to both of them—married and single. Whichever you are—and you must be one or the other, if you like it or not—you have a feeling that you have that word branded somewhere. That it could be removed seems a remote possibility; that it could be removed and replaced again at some point, smacks of highly improbable fiction. The thing is, though, that we are not actually branded with the word beyond being labeled as such on driver's licenses and other government and work records. The thing is, though, that it is really fairly easy, at any time in your adult life, to slip back and forth between the two states. And, to make life an even more unsettled proposition, there are times when people are involved in a kind of legal limbo, where they are living the single life but still on the books as married; waiting for a divorce to be final or just cheating. Or living in every way as a married couple, except for being married.

Throwing the situation into total chaos, even a good marriage is subject to periods of aloneness for both partners—sometimes while they are in the same room, on the same couch. These lulls or brief separations (including such as occur on a daily basis through work) are short but not-to-be-ignored phases of the single life.

What am I driving at? Simply this: that married people must not consider themselves rescued from the single life—they live it part-time daily and could easily make a full return to it once or several times before the end. And you singles too. You're probably not going to stay that way! It's all illusion! So—whoever you are—prepare yourself for both states!

Part 3: Making the Single Life a Good Thing

(The Unmarried) dream away their time without friendship, without fondness, and are driven to rid themselves of the day, for which they have no use, by childish amusements or vicious delights. They act as beings under the constant sense of some known inferiority, that fills their minds with rancor and their tongues with censure. They are peevish at home and malevolent abroad; and, as the outlaws of human nature, make it their business and their pleasure to disturb that society which debars them from its privileges.

—Samuel Johnson, writer

33.

Destroying the Image

Everybody around us seems to be part of a conspiracy to make us feel deep down that being uninvolved romantically during a certain age range (say 18 to 50) is reason for depression. In movies, television, and all too often in real life news stories, the loner is depicted as one not only without happiness but with special problems. The loner—usually someone reduced to this state by either a broken or hopeless love affair—becomes (if a man) a drifter drug addict alcohol abuser murderer, often all four simultaneously; the woman becomes an eccentric, either a total recluse or just quirky, or eventually commits suicide. And of course loners, or soon-to-be loners, of both sexes are versatile revenge takers, women's stock in trade ranging from the traditional sneaky (poison in the coffee) to the modern to-the-point (cutting it off); men's ranging from straightforward extreme violence (beating with fists) to straightforward extremer violence (disturbing her at work with an assault rifle).

We get a less exaggerated or extreme picture from the rare people who actually pass through our lives that we know or can see to be loners. They have—or appear to have—sad eyes, permanent frowns, a generally somewhat unkempt appearance, and unattractive auras. We are embarrassed for them when we see them sitting wrapped in over-abundant elbow room in restaurants, movie theaters, nightclubs. If they laugh loudly and smile widely during the movie, eat heartily at the restaurant, have an energetic dance at the nightclub, the first thought is "How pitiful, this must be their only pleasure in life."

But this may not be true. Sometimes people that go alone to movies restaurants and nightclubs are simply people who are between

Part 3: Making the Single Life a Good Thing

relationships—people who have learned to relax and enjoy themselves while they are single. So much so that they sometimes feel the presence of a friend to be an unnecessary security blanket and choose to go alone. There are of course the ones who are not comfortable with their singleness, who are driven out by desperate loneliness, not being able to stand their empty houses or apartments for another minute. But the point is that we, all of us as we are growing up, see both kinds as pathetic due to cultural stereotyping.

I'm sure that even most of those loners who enjoy themselves much of the time they are alone still have a degree of self-suspicion about their normality. Maybe they even suspect they are a little crazy, not being depressed because they "ain't got nobody." After all, there is no escaping the daily tide of images, sweeping over us through television magazines and every other form of media including video games; and in the real world, flooding over us virtually the moment we open the front door. These images are so familiar, and so steady is their procession, that our awareness of their significance is almost entirely on the subconscious level.

When we see commercials clearly meant to portray people having a good time they almost always (it's true there are those 4x4 driving adds with both men and women happily tearing up the countryside solo) feature couples. Sometimes they show several couples, or an assortment of men and women not clearly paired but easy to imagine that some of them either are or could get together. The same goes for magazine adds. And as for the real world, a single glance at one green light's worth of thoroughfare traffic provides glimpses of a legion of family-designed vehicles.

All of this brainwashing amounts to a formidable opponent, in fact a Goliath—but you know what a David, if only he is well-armed in bravery, rocks and a sling will do to a Goliath. There is no greater power in the arguments of a giant just because he is big. Perhaps a greater noise, a more permeating breath, and a more intimidating stare, but not often as solid a logical basis of reasons as those spoken quietly by a shrewd David. Many of the people who form the gigantic body of couples may show a blustering (or at least smugly smiling) complacency

Happy Between Relationships

with their couple status when among people they know, and yet be terribly bored or otherwise miserable when together in private.

As for all the terribly bored or otherwise miserable single people out there, it is my opinion that they have bought into the flashy public appearance of couples, not caring to notice signs of sub-satisfaction. Often they even forget their own miserable relationships of the past, only remembering the few highlights they contained. This alluring flash of couples would be rendered far less blinding if only the miserable single knew an interesting truth: he or she has actually a better chance of being happy than the couple!

Yes, I say this without hesitation, without reservation. There is no doubt in my mind, from my personal experiences of both happy couplehood and happy singlehood, that the happy odds are stacked in the favor of the single—if only the single realizes singlehood can be exploited for happiness and can find a plan for doing so. But this is not just my experience.

For their book *Flying Solo: Single Women in Midlife,* Carol Anderson, Ph.D., Susan Stewart, Ph.D., and Sona Dimidjian, M. S. W., questioned 50 single women about their lives. This survey, compared with surveys of married women, suggested that "women tend to live longer, are happier, and accomplish more professionally when they are single." The funny thing is that men, according to Dr. Stewart, tend to find life tough going when they are unmarried. Being a man myself who has enjoyed my singlehood, I nonetheless think I can understand some of the reasons behind this. And I venture to guess many are just an extension of the pressures that cause large numbers of young and youngish people of both sexes anxiety about their single status and often to accept bad matches for marriage.

Marriage, as I shall always believe in the face of any negative stats, can still be the crowning joy of life for a substantial percentage of the population. However, it adds much complexity to the balancing act of life. It requires for success skill *and* luck: you must be lucky enough to meet a good match and skillful enough to develop it *and* yourself at the same time. However, it is possible to simplify things quite a bit by

Part 3: Making the Single Life a Good Thing

taking advantage of singlehood to develop your happiness. It only takes the belief that it can be done and the putting into practice the ideas in this book. Then, if you are lucky enough to find a good match, you will only have to work to develop your relationship—you yourself will be solid and prepared for any malfunction in the relationship. Read on to find many more techniques for developing resources to construct a happiness that has nothing to do with luck or fate and cannot be damaged by the behavior of others.

34.

About my Own Happy Aloneness

✵

I myself—and this is no boast—am one of the better living examples of someone who has been happy between relationships. But not only that; I have been in a fairly extreme isolation by necessity, and for a number of years. The reason might be guessed; because I tell you this through a book. My choice of profession was writing fiction, made in my late teens, and to this I geared my education—writing books, not teaching, was all I wanted to do. This was not hard to make a living doing—or perhaps wouldn't have been if it had only been possible to get my books published.

Therefore I have had to live as best I could, getting money to survive by ways other than the one I preferred: part-time projects, jobs, and the generosity of my family. The reason I don't make it my boast that I was and am able to find happiness on a meager income is that I would, even now, have wanted circumstances to have been different. That is, I would have loved—all the time I was happy as a proverbial lark—to have had the money to get married, or at least to date enough to have a chance to meet another girl with whom I was as well-matched as my first love. "Wait a minute," someone might say, "how could you have been happy and dissatisfied at the same time? You're contradicting yourself." I answer this charge of contradiction with contradiction: "No I'm not!"

This is because I was not dissatisfied. In fact I was highly satisfied. "Wait a minute," someone may say again tenaciously, "you're picking on the word 'dissatisfied'—you know what I'm getting at!" Yes I think I do; and what I wrote covers that meaning as well—I was happy, entirely, really happy. The tenacious one hangs on: " Well, how can

Part 3: Making the Single Life a Good Thing

that be?" I'm happy, if you'll excuse the expression, to answer. It comes down to the fortunate circumstance that, while I would have loved to be in love and having a career breakthrough, I loved what I had just as much. And what I had that I loved was, for the most part, no more than what anybody could have.

This is why it seemed to me that I might have stumbled on a valuable formula for living. If a person struggling with a series of major career setbacks, living on the edge financially, all the while without romantic comforts and moral support, *and* without the prospect of any of this changing in the near future—if this person can be happy anyone can.

Now, what were these magical secrets for happiness I had discovered in my adversity? Did they have to do with my work of writing novels? As a matter of fact they did have to do with my career—but they were far from being magic and far from being applicable only to novelists. These 'secrets' were nothing but the by-products of an artist's mind-set. Not specifically the act of writing a novel; or for that matter painting a picture or doing any other kind of artwork. What I mean by 'artist's mind-set' is the unified state of mind where everything you see is seen as a potential tool of creation, as raw material; not necessarily for the creation of art*work* but, quite realistically, for the creation of life *as* art. (More on the artist's mind-set in Part 4.)

35.

Meaning Equals Excitement

With those who have been plagued with a sense of meaninglessness in relationships and life in general, and feel that being on their own would make life too bleak to bear, I would humbly beg to differ. Being on their own could be the way to the revelation they have been searching for. The start is allowing yourself to relax and look around you, rather than just staying busy in a thoughtless way, keeping the air cluttered with distracting noises and chat. Once you are positioned to think without rush or racket, and are willing to let go of the fear of what you might find there, a moment of great possibilities is at hand. After soon finding that your fears do not have the power to strike you dead on the spot, I believe you are presented with a choice of two mental directions.

The first is the old one, which would be chosen largely as a residue of dismal night thoughts, of listing all the aspects of an empty and threatening world. As the result, in other words, of treading the long, circular and deeply well-worn path of a laundry list of little worries. Which includes, among a cast of thousands:

- Getting sick.
- Having to deal with a certain person or situation at work.
- Being late.
- Getting enough sleep.
- Losing your job.
- Paying bills.
- And on and on.

These worries are chosen as a result of the consequent blindness to all that currently surrounds you and the possibilities these things suggest.

Part 3: Making the Single Life a Good Thing

Such a mental path has no use other than to take you on a mad roller coaster ride with no end and nothing but one harrowing descent after another and no uphill parts on which to recover. This is the inward direction of gnawing, overdone fears.

The second direction is to open your eyes and step out of yourself. Say this quiet moment of thought is taking place in a garden. Well what better place to step out of yourself into! Opening not only your eyes but all your other senses as well, diving into the details, wallowing in the details, you can finally really see the garden. Instead of playing the role of a background prop to your endless interior monologue performance, the garden sweeps forward. Pushing you off stage into the first row, you are lost in the shadows while a natural vision dazzles under the lights. In such dazzling mini-spectacles as a dew-hung spider web, a gust setting off a ten thousand leaf dance, a bright flower emulating the sun, there is far more productive food for speculation than there is relating to yourself and your worries.

This sort of discovery can also be the start of a new injection of meaning into your life.

However, you must remember that certain essentials must be in place for sustained meaningful living:

- Self-love.

- Love of a fair number of things in the world of any kind, whether animal, vegetable, mineral or otherwise.

- At least one pursuit that you are passionate about and that can be practiced daily in some form.

And I will add that each item of this list tends to foster and produce the others. For example, achievements in the area of your passionate pursuit will increase self-love, as will also your caring about things other than just what concerns you.

Let's explore how these and other goals might be achieved.

36.

Defining Goals for the Single Life—and Accomplishing Them

Goals may be of practically any size and so you can work towards goals and achieve them (smaller ones) all day long. This will establish a mind-set in which achieving larger ones will become natural. Make everything you possibly can into a goal which you know you can achieve with a little effort, and make sure you put out the effort required and achieve that goal every time. After a while make it a little harder each time and do whatever it takes but do it—you can because it's just a tiny additional effort required. For example, you might try getting up five minutes earlier every morning for a couple of weeks; this not only provides a goal achievement right out of the starting gate but gives you additional time before work to dedicate to your projects. But remember that every goal you set is just as important as any other and that the achievement of the ones you hold dear is only to be reached by the stepping stones of the everyday variety.

Your projects are what make being single a delicious exciting time in your life. What should they be? How do you know the one you choose is the right one? How ambitious should it be? Answering the third question answers all three. High ambition is essential; the higher the better. This means you should shoot for no less than greatness, fame, and riches or whatever are the ultimate rewards of success in the field whose work you feel you would *enjoy* doing more than any other—not necessarily the one typically bringing the most money or celebrity. This does not mean, however, that you should aim immediately to become president of the United States if your dream job would be that of a politician. And yet it does not mean that you should not have the ultimate aim of becoming President. You work by stages, starting, say, as a

Part 3: Making the Single Life a Good Thing

candidate for the city council and move up when you're ready and the opportunity offers; and if indeed you are serious about wanting to become President, then most likely you will be more ready and more look the part of the Golden Child to be groomed for higher office than the members of council who have more modest goals.

37.

The Case for Being Single: the Arguments, the Reasons

Being single, for a few months or even a few years, can be a wonderful liberating experience. It can be what is widely supposed to be only attainable through love affairs and marriages: freedom to really live. It *can* be freedom to:

- focus on developing yourself;
- make a full-force commitment to advancing your career;
- socialize with or date a wide variety of people;
- go anywhere you want and do anything you want whenever you want to.

All this while keeping an eye open for someone who might be a good match.

The picture people have of someone who is alone is usually not a pretty one. They imagine a grim guy or gal, sitting in front of the TV eating junk food for comfort, a dazed look in their eyes, the corners of their mouth imperceptibly working downward into a permanent frown. My personal picture of an unattached person would be something on the lines of the following: a robust figure tan from indulging in outdoor and sporting activities, on the way downtown to hit the shops and people-watch before going to a play or concert, after a morning spent in the library and local park researching for a project or just reading for fun or to become more knowledgeable. Why does a person who is alone have to be down in the mouth, their life on hold or, in the case of someone over fifty, in essence over? Why must this person wait and hope for someone who is willing to attach themselves to them, as though they

Part 3: Making the Single Life a Good Thing

were an amputee waiting for prosthetic legs?

The arguments for remaining without a break in intimate companionship with the various social combinations were a lot stronger in the distant past. When humankind was young hairy inarticulate and impolite, a real social disgrace in fact, their life circumstances were even ruder and more cutthroat than they are today if you can believe it. They were forced, as unsightly as were their smiles and foul their breath, to cling together constantly in range of those breaths for protection against ever-threatening danger. Love, if it existed then, would have been a remote factor in maintaining these tight groups of relations. More practical ones such as the need for someone to watch your back to keep lions off it, or the need for several young and strong bodies to form effective hunting or gathering parties must have topped the list. Mating and sex were strictly family considerations, the creation of a family group being motivated again primarily by numbers considerations; the mystical desire to reproduce themselves of course forming part of it. I do not think the idea of willfully separating themselves from any one of these connections ever popped into any Neanderthal skull: without them their chances of surviving two weeks longer would have been reduced to about zero.

For the modern person, however, even if he or she is hairy inarticulate and impolite, the imperative has been taken out of the need which everybody feels from time to time for the various social groupings. If we choose we may step outside the intimacy of these kinds of social circles for a given period without the likelihood of dying from it or even being maimed—psychologically or otherwise. The reason that many people go their entire lifetime without ever becoming alone as a *deliberate* choice...and feel as though they are hardly alive when not involved with somebody...is that they never realized that there are equally rich life experiences to be had when on their own—and, more importantly, only when on their own.

38.

Advantages of Being Unattached

※

There are interesting arguments for being single indefinitely. Even if you are aware of them, though, the largely irrational demands of your biological nature will likely ignore them at one point or another for a shorter or longer period, whether the situation is ideal or not, for the sake of a family. Let us explore them anyway.

You are never obliged to remain in a state of intimacy with someone. When you're single, perhaps dating once in awhile, you only interact socially or intimately with someone when you feel like doing so. When you're married or in a relationship, almost inevitably there are evenings when being with that person, just being subjected to their well-meaning presence, is a bore. In the case of marriage, if the match isn't an extraordinarily good one, it doesn't take long before evenings become predictable, your partner either becoming a dull rock of dependability or a volatile nightmare. When you're single you need never be bored by anybody:

- if you begin to bore yourself you can pick up a book by an interesting person (like me!);
- put it down when you've had enough;
- go see a friend with whom you have catching up to do;
- come home and turn on the late news to be informed about the fresh doings of people you don't know much if anything about.

All without the accompaniment of a person you possibly know more than you want to about, who to top it off doesn't have much or anything new to say to you.

Part 3: Making the Single Life a Good Thing

I don't say it's this terrible in all relationships, just the poor or mediocre matches. And yet even in dynamic relationships there are less awful versions of the above, ruts and dead spots that are pretty easily outweighed by the good times. But when you're single you need *never* be bored to tears with a person.

More advantages of being unattached

The extra time you have to devote to your career and hobbies. Let's face it, relationships require an enormous investment of your time. Even a halfhearted relationship destined to hit a dead end gobbles up prime hours of leisure time, which might otherwise have been put to constructive use. And in order to make a promising relationship succeed there must be a mutual commitment of almost every non-working non-sleeping hour to some form of activity which might strengthen the bond—whether it is going out or relaxing together at home or long talks on the phone or writing letters or just thinking about them and wondering if and what they're thinking about you.

And, of course, if you get married and decide to have children right away, there goes all but a few drops of time to work on your dreams and passions for a few years, especially if you're a woman. (Unless of course you find raising babies is your passion, in which case you're in luck.)

On the other hand, if you choose to socialize sporadically or not at all, you find that not only do projects and goals begin popping into your mind with only the slightest assistance. Also, even more miraculously, you find there is substantial time to work on them. And, perhaps best of all, there are no interruptions—not even the phone if you've overdone it. In fact you may find that, on top of being able to devote quality time to the pursuit of your career dreams, there is also ample time to relax and even indulge in a spell of guilt-free laziness after. At the same time, of course, there is the inevitability that you will have nothing but time to feel lonely if you find you don't desire anything beyond romantic love and a family; but I think most everyone has something they truly enjoy aside from relationships: it just needs to be recognized and developed.

Happy Between Relationships

When you are single you are likely to save money. Once again facing the coldhearted facts, even if you tend to be a spendthrift it's hard to spend a lot of money when you're single. Going to fancy restaurants, seeing movies in the theaters, going on elaborate weekend outings, buying new clothes, gifts, things in general—the rate at which these activities occur falls off dramatically. Instead you tend to dine out less and when you do it's at less ritzy places, rent movies, refrain from packing the weekends with status-oriented high-ticket events, and buy only when a thing is necessary and not to impress. What savings are possible can be astounding, largely because it is so easy to spend all extra money available through the natural urge not to seem tightfisted. (I am referring equally to men and women here because with most women working today and many in high positions the old man-pays-for-everything is quickly becoming an insult.)

Part 3: Making the Single Life a Good Thing

Sex is the Tabasco sauce which an adolescent national palate sprinkles on every course in the menu.

—Mary Day Winn, writer

Never play cards with any man named "Doc."

Never eat at any place called "Mom's"

And never, never, no matter what else you do in your whole life, never sleep with anyone whose troubles are worse than your own.

—Nelson Algren, novelist

39.

Taking a Break from Sex

Believe it or not, *not* having sex is one of the most refreshing things about being between relationships. That is, again, for persons who have somehow been able to quiet the voices of movie and TV characters and certain boastful friends echoing in their heads, and consider that such a thing is possible. Once the process of questioning has begun, however briefly, it is quite likely that at least some passing doubt will creep in as to the need to be constantly having sex in order to be happy. And for those who continue to take serious thought on the subject, it will become clearer and clearer that there may be some truth here. Don't get me wrong; I love sex; and, so I've been told by a few partners, I provide ample thrills. So what I'm writing isn't from the point of view of a blah sex life; nor do I have cause to be blase, not having had scads of lovers.

Upon the ending of a sexual relationship, instead of missing the act, think about your new freedom. Everyone is a virtual slave to a common assortment of things in a normal life, e.g. work food drink and so on, and no doubt sex appears to most everyone one of the most appealing of slave drivers. But freedom from it for a time can be particularly advantageous. It releases the spirit in a number of ways:

> • You are not so much subject to the call of the animal or 'lizard' brain, making you something of a less irrational emotional creature.

> • You are empowered by the feeling that you can do what you want instead of being like a robot programmed to seek sex.

> • Your brain is less cluttered (notice I don't say uncluttered)

Part 3: Making the Single Life a Good Thing

with sexual imagery from anticipating when and where you'll 'do it' today.

It's a healthy exercise to look at sex for what it really is (excluding those times when it is the expression of love at its height) to keep overrating it to a minimum. I think many people will agree that it frequently serves the following functions, sometimes combined with love and sometimes not: relieving tension, an escape from the worries of the day, a way to avoid conversation in general or a given problem in particular, something to do, satisfying a generic desire for an orgasm, an outlet for anger, exercise. Apart from the motivation for having sex, there is the act itself; not a particularly fascinating thing when pondered without heat: bamm bamm bamm bamm (and now for variation) slam slam slam slam (and now for the big finale) squirt! Sex is also not particularly:

- lasting
- dependable
- productive
- safe

I want to repeat, however, that sex, used right, is a tremendous boon not only to love but to health. Nevertheless looking at its inglorious side is quite necessary to assign sex a proper value and prevent it from assuming monstrous dimensions in your life. And it's quite clear that for many of the uses sex is commonly put to, as listed above, more creative and productive alternatives can be found.

40.

The Benefit for Women of Being Temporarily Unattached

※

As a man I find it somewhat painful to admit that men are often brutish towards women, and that women, though performing in many cases non-angelic acts with high frequency, are almost always far more civilized in their treatment of their partner, even when it comes to doing him wrong. It's my theory that this is largely a simple matter of the big and muscular one bullying the small non-muscular one; that if women were bigger and more muscular than men they would behave like men and men like women. Since, however, most women are not comparable to their men in strength, women might do well to shun men with brutish tendencies and learn to wait patiently unattached for the man who combines backbone with gentleness—and I do believe there is a small to medium-sized contingent of them currently in circulation. And yet this 'patient wait' needn't be of the meek waiting-to-get-a-life variety. It's an exciting opportunity to build:

- strength
- wisdom

and an extra room as it were, precisely the way one is added to a house, where you might establish a semi-private workshop whose designs become as precious to you as any social happiness the living room and bedroom may have seen.

For a woman there are some extra benefits to be had from being without a relationship (either a heterosexual or homosexual one). I'll start with the most fundamental physical fact: she is in a position to orchestrate such things as nightly entertainment and weekend excursions completely

Part 3: Making the Single Life a Good Thing

on her own; and, more importantly, embark upon them without a romantic companion. Of course this was at least a conceivable operation while in the relationship, but awkward because it might have taken some convincing of innocent intentions to put down suspicions of unfaithfulness. And by nightly entertainment I don't mean just watching sitcoms or renting videos; nor by weekend excursions do I mean just going shopping. It seems to me that it must necessarily be a terrific empowerment for a woman to take herself on a bold flight into the deep dark evening. She and a friend might stop at a nightclub, and find that, instead of worrying that people will think they are sluts or that men will make aggressive advances, she feels the confidence springing from her aggressive independence that will allow her to deal easily with either situation.

Similarly, say she takes a long weekend drive into the mountains or to the beach. The difference that exists between being a passenger under the protective wing of a man (or that of the dominant partner in a lesbian relationship) and being the driver at the wheel of control is a world's worth. You go from being a passive one, hands meekly folded in the lap, looking now helplessly at the scenery now admiringly or shyly at the one trusted with your life—to a person dominating a burly horsepower beast, driving it relentlessly forward with your foot while flexing you're biceps as you crank the wheel on sharp turns.

A woman oftentimes is too ready to give up the more masculine aspects of her personality to either satisfy her man's urges for total control or because she has convinced herself she's better off without their burden. I think, on the other hand, that certain kinds of behavior, that I will term masculine if only because they have traditionally been seen as such, are simply essential for inexhaustible happiness. These include:

- decisiveness;
- holding strong opinions;
- being adventurous;
- taking minor risks;
- being ambitious;
- fighting back.

Happy Between Relationships

Without these kinds of aggression (and I mean these specific kinds—I don't think a full page would be space enough for the list of *bad* kinds of typical male aggression) a woman is dependent on someone else. A husband boyfriend or children are relied on to provide their pleasures and prevent people from taking advantage of them and sadnesses devastating them—none of which they can really do anyway. With these qualities sad eventualities and even catastrophes will not devastate the spirit; and quite possibly these setbacks will become added motivation to become stronger and yet more purposeful.

Thus a divorce, or two or three divorces, the children growing up and leaving, a husband dying prematurely or in ripe years, a longtime boyfriend suddenly leaving you; even such initial horrors as becoming paralyzed from the neck down or such permanent ones as having someone in the family murdered: terribly hard as they all are to deal with, they are contingencies that the strong aggressive person can make themselves face defiantly before during and after they befall them, spitting into the teeth of the monster the words, "I will not be reduced except by death—give me your best shot."

Part 3: Making the Single Life a Good Thing

Married in haste, we may repent at leisure.

—William Congreve, playwright

When a match has equal partners, then I fear not.

—Aeschylus, playwright

41.

Using the Single Life to Make Sure You Avoid Getting into Abusive Relationships

Many marriages and relationships feature an abusive aspect. And whether physical or psychological, the one doing the more violent types of each is usually the man—of course. He has the muscle and, in the majority of cases, the money. And surprisingly, according to Pat Lanning, district director of Family and Children's Services, "The more powerful the man, the more likely he is to feel above the law and inflict abuse." And this abuse is often severe and vicious on top of being widespread (according to the FBI one out of every four women will be physically assaulted by a man she's lived with at some point in her life). So severe that 2000 women a year are killed by it; so vicious that pregnancy actually increases a woman's chance of being beaten.

So why do women put up with this? Whatever the reasons, whether for the children's sake, because they have no money of their own, perverse love—they shouldn't. But what they really shouldn't was to have gotten into the abusive relationship in the first place. Easier said than done? Maybe, but I think the odds of staying out of them go way up if two things are true: that the woman is very happy in her life between relationships; and that the man whom she eventually pegs as a good match for her is also *already* very happy.

This situation has the following effect when they get together. The bottom line is that if the relationship dies, even after going as far as marriage, even after going as far as children, happiness will likely display resilience. After all, if you had been happy before, solidly happy aside from any romantic interest, what is lacking to make it up again? How can it ever really cease? Romantic love, if never viewed as

Part 3: Making the Single Life a Good Thing

necessary to meaningful essential living, can never make life meaningless by ending—as the robot in *Lost in Space* used to say: "That does not compute!"

But the effect of two people being quite happy going into a relationship is at least as interesting as its effect on them coming out. In fact so interesting that the chances are they may never come out. It has two dynamic consequences that are almost inevitable:

> 1) Since the couple do not depend on each other, but welcome each other, for making the time interesting and fulfilling, there are fewer demands placed on each other. Fewer demands means less tension and fewer arguments, and any disagreements will likely be resolved without violent emotion.
>
> 2) They will inevitably have much more to say to each other of a positive non-complaining nature; and this energizing kind of conversation will likely continue at a brisk rate indefinitely. Why so? Because what made them happy before they were a couple, if smartly continued into the relationship, will supply regular gold strikes of conversational nuggets, to be mined at leisure. And these nuggets would consist of the exciting new discoveries bound to result with reasonable regularity to people who apply a consistent passion toward achieving some object in the field of learning. Learning of almost any kind, really. A happy person is someone who is learning *something* all the time, to oversimplify a bit. Even happier if your learning—your passion—can be turned into a career or some kind of creative project.

42.

Taking People or Leaving Them

I love people. I love them in every possible incarnation: both male and female, young and old, white black brown yellow, smart and not-so-smart, tall short average height, beautiful or handsome or not-so-beautiful or handsome, subtle or obvious, etc. And they interest me, though I may not always love them, in every possible role: father mother wife husband son daughter; burglar war-hero lawyer juggler actor janitor President of the U.S.A. and so forth. And yet I can take people or leave them; take them joyfully or leave them without lingering sadness. And this truly is one of the most key abilities you need not only to be happy for yourself, but to be able to spread happiness to others. It may sound coldhearted, uncaring, unloving, perhaps inhuman, to some people, but it is really the opposite.

The person who will not let go in a relationship, who says they will forever remain devoted to a person no matter what, is setting themselves up for a lesser or greater disaster. For a starter I would never devote myself to another person; any relationship, whether between parent and child or husband and wife, should proceed on the basis of equality and devotion is slavish. There must be an understanding that all the courtesy and respect common at first introduction between strangers must be upheld to some degree continually; if disrespect crops up in any form even in very small doses it must stop or the relationship must stop. Because no happiness can exist for the abused and none but that of abusing for the abuser. This may mean a suspension of the relationship while the abusing party comes to realize and reform his or her mistakes; or a permanent end to intimacy—which may be the wiser course as abuse, while it may be checked for awhile, usually reappears once the abuser feels secure again.

Part 3: Making the Single Life a Good Thing

Once a tie of intimacy has been cleanly broken, there is absolutely no need to succumb to the onslaught of those cold, empty, lonely feelings—which always end up prompting you to go scampering back. But its not enough merely to seek out a series of diversions to take the mind off the person in question. Nor is surrounding yourself with friends a real remedy. Even realizing that there are many fish in the sea and that you're bound to land a good one with persistence, though a healthy positive outlook, does little for you in the short term—which, let's face it, may not be so short. With no better alternatives than these, even if a return to the abusive situation is avoided, the likelihood is great that some other faulty relationship will be substituted for it if nothing better offers. Unquestionably what is needed is the ability to feel comfortable without constant intimacy. The ability to find happiness through your own pursuits, with your interactions with others such as friends lovers and relatives forming single courses of the seven course feasts you create on your own. Then there is independence in the most positive sense possible. This way all other people, including those most worthy of your affection, assume the aspect of a mere plus in your life, to be discarded with relative ease if the writing's on the wall.

Let's look at how to lay the spiritual groundwork for this comfort.

43.

Reinforcing and Polishing Your Spirit

※

Finding yourself alone and summoning the bravery to look steadily into the eyes of that bogeymen and finding no tragic depths—just the harmless far-off gaze of a bugbear—the result is likely to be the onset of a potentially very useful feeling of tranquillity. Now I know that tranquillity seems pretty useless except for the purposes of a brief rest; but I am referring to a particular kind of tranquillity. The kind where the quality of tranquillity is ever-present and yet easily dispersed in its surface layers to make room for agitated creative moods and such—yet always in the background of your feelings, like lush stage scenery. With your life clear of the inevitable emotional clutter related to a partner's presence, you become free to develop a continual connection with your own spirit in this inner tranquillity. It's a golden chance to grow your spirit, your potential to react spiritually to what stimulates you in life.

The spirit is really not such a mystical indefinable thing as it may seem. Whatever else it may be, it is the great gushing well of such productive things as hope ambition wonder love, running clean and contemptuous of any pollutants opposed to the fulfilling happy life. But, just like any other wellspring, it requires maintenance to ensure that it does not dry up. And what better time to undertake such a beneficial—and most enjoyable in itself—task than when between relationships. And yet cleaning the spirit is a more complex operation than unclogging a wellspring, the spirit being itself a complex and strange piece of nature: delicate as a mist yet as intense and persistent as an everlasting bonfire; elusive and yet all-pervading; long-winded on love and hope, silent on hate and despair; happy for everyone if happy for itself. Still, in spite of this strangeness, I will not call it mystic in the sense of nearly

Part 3: Making the Single Life a Good Thing

inscrutable; to me it speaks in tongues of a higher logic, that of general love. It speaks of:

- the exciting possibilities of the single life.

The possibility to explore:

1) the world inside you;
2) the world outside you.

Now cleaning repairing and growing the spirit is not only a good thing for the long run, but it also can be a delicious medicine. Nor does it need to be a monotonous cure. Spirit repairs, as well as the application of a polish, might consist of a wide range of activities. Of course what works in anything always varies from individual to individual, but here is an example of a simple activity that should be an effective chiropractor for the elusive bones of the spirit-being for most, especially the unattached:

Walking in the park. Now this needn't be only the simple enjoyment of a reminder of nature balanced by a reminder of humanity's golden age (where everybody was apparently a shepherd or married to one, and thus spent a lot of time lying on the grass or propped against shade trees). For example, shaking off the golden age dreaminess and merely taking an observant stroll past the various park seating arrangements, such as benches and barbecue tables, cannot fail to be spiritually uplifting. That is if what you are likely to see is viewed with the proper attitude for someone who is on their own. Remember that the spirit thrives on a positive attitude. (And if I haven't repeated myself on this point yet let me do so now: *you* thrive on a positive attitude as well, yes, your entire package of spirit, body, mind, pocketbook, prospects both social and career—so accentuate it, just as the song says!).

Now, armed with this powerful positive attitude, you may stroll past these benches and feel something a lot like elfish glee. For when you see the cozy young couple engaged in alternating nuzzling and nestling, you have found an aid to imagining and anticipating your own next

Happy Between Relationships

love affair; and if you are well removed from youth, there is spiritual growth to be had in shunning thoughts of jealousy and comparing the high points of your own past loves and aspiring to the rare and admirable feat of a youthful love affair in your later years.

On the next bench you see a couple having a quarrelsome-looking argument about something which you immediately feel is trivially domestic. In this case you are justified in feeling the full complement of tingly sensations because you are free and clear of such a phase in a relationship—where your partner has been somehow transformed into a mosquito that it's illegal to swat. The same goes for the next bench where the couple you see appear to vaguely know each other, judging by the remotely intimate distance between their bodies of about a foot, but otherwise seem to be oblivious, or trying to be oblivious, of the other's presence. And there is nothing mean-spirited in this. You are merely appreciating your carefree independence and position on the edge of the fresh beginning of your next relationship, however distant it may be; you are not glad that these people are unhappy, it is to be hoped that they will recognize that it is time to part company and get on with positive living.

And as for the benches occupied by singles of various types—readers, blank gazers, grim thinkers, dull ruminators, cheerful watchers, lonely yearners—the spirit soars at the thought that you are light and free and stripped of the heaviness of some; especially, however, at the thought that those that appear content to be on their own are perhaps people in a similar stage in life to yours, also able to appreciate their freedom.

Part 3: Making the Single Life a Good Thing

You're not just sleeping with one person, you're sleeping with everyone *they* ever slept with.

—Theresa Crenshaw, writer

44.

Dealing with AIDS and Venereal Disease

The benefits of being between relationships are many and for the most part boil down to giving you time and uncluttered mental space in which to explore and develop yourself and your potential and opportunities— and to find the most valuable thing there is: ways to enjoy your own company. After all, you are the person you are married to in the strict sense. I think the words spoken in the wedding ceremony as marriage vows would be far more appropriate for an obstetrician to say to the person he is bringing into the world. With some slight editing, they would go from expressing the improbable to an eloquent representation of an absolute truth. "Whether you solemnly swear or not, you will take this life, for richer or poorer, in sickness and in health, till death do you part." There is no possibility of divorce or even separation, you have to find a way to make it work. The compensation for this grim life sentence is that you are dealing with a person who will always communicate their feelings, who knows you intimately, and who sincerely always wants a reconciliation.

These are the spiritual reasons why being between relationships can be beneficial to your lifelong happiness. However, being between relationships can also be beneficial to your health, and thus give yet another boost to your happiness.

I might just as well be referring to the benefits of establishing an exercise routine between relationships, but I am not (see section on exercise in Part 5). In fact the benefit I am about to describe is the opposite of exercise in a way, which is one of the highest forms of positive action you can take to recover and move rapidly forward after a breakup. This benefit is passive and a denial of a spicy pleasure of life—and yet it

Part 3: Making the Single Life a Good Thing

can be even more important than exercise for both physical and mental health. I'm talking about the total certainty you will not get AIDS or any of the assortment of venereal diseases when you are abstaining from sexual relationships. Exercise may truly be a panacea, but I think most would agree that it is preferable to use it to build a positive self image, strength and good feelings than for fighting for your life.

As I write it is 1997 and the AIDS epidemic is still raging through the world, and likely to continue to rage for the foreseeable future. Even though the introduction of a line of protease inhibitor drugs has been able to reduce the virus to undetectable levels in the blood of some patients, there is still no cure and no vaccine. Perhaps "we're seeing the start of a steady decline" in deaths due to AIDS in the United States, as Dr. Steve Schnittman of the National Institute of Allergy and Infectious Diseases was quoted as thinking. Yet the cost of the assortment of drugs required to keep levels down is $20,000 for a year's supply. And in Africa and South and Southeast Asia the number of the infected is still increasing at a bacterial rate with 95% of the sufferers without access to drug treatment and unable to pay for it if they could get it. And if they could get the drugs and pay for them, they would still have to be able to tolerate the strong side effects (which some of those who can afford them here can't do) and the knowledge that the virus could resurface in a more powerful form.

This means that AIDS will be something worth taking seriously into consideration when thinking of becoming intimate with anyone for a long time to come. Even if they find a vaccine and you are duly vaccinated, would it be a comfortable proposition to put your faith in it? If it is well-proven, maybe. Maybe not. Anyway there is no vaccine, just an epidemic. And a deadly epidemic, though slowly declining, is still a deadly epidemic, and in spite of the decline in the number who die the percentage of women infected continues to rise. With the numbers of infected skyrocketing in other countries, and American's continuing to go abroad, and foreigners continuing to be allowed in (as they should), there will be plenty of it around no matter how well we control our domestic variety.

Just as bad as actually catching the disease is the idea that we have

Happy Between Relationships

joined a risk group for catching it. When you are a promiscuous gay male, it goes without saying that you live each day in a terror of gnawing anxiety. The same nightmare applies to IV drug users, though they may find a retreat from it when they are high. But these are people in high-risk groups. The risk groups I referred to still include everybody who indulges in sexual flings, in spite of the fact that the explosion predicted in the 80's of heterosexual transmission never occurred. Having a sexual relationship with someone you have taken the time to get to know and feel certain they neither take IV drugs or are cheating on you with gay men, is probably pretty safe—though a condom is always a good idea. Promiscuity, on the other hand, even with condoms, is real danger *and* anxiety hell, not much different really than being in the high-risk group. Regarding anxiety about their promiscuity, any promiscuous person who has heard of Magic Johnson contracting AIDS must be racked with it. Being nervous all the time is no way to find true happiness.

Therefore a good way to ensure a clear working surface on which to build happiness between relationships is not to be promiscuous after a breakup. Nor is it any tragedy to be sexually inactive between relationships. Aside from it sometimes actually being refreshing not to be involved sexually (see Chapter "Taking a break from sex" earlier in this Part), it is peaceful. By this I mean that not only do you become incapable of worrying about contracting HIV, you become incapable of worrying about contracting herpes, gonorrhea, and all the rest of those lovelies. Why? Because you know the odds of your testing positive for any of these without sexual contact are fairly well against it—something like 10,000 to 1. Unless of course you're an IV drug user, or work in a hospital and tend to inadvertently jab yourself with needles connected to syringes full of AIDS-tainted blood. Even if, against all odds, you are carrying dormant HIV from a previous relationship, at least you have no current possible exposures for the back of your mind to chew nervously like a piece of meat you suspect may contain a bone. Let yourself savor in a relaxed atmosphere this new course in your life so as to get its full, rich flavor.

Part 3: Making the Single Life a Good Thing

I don't need a man to rectify my existence. The most profound relationship we'll ever have is the one with ourselves.

—Shirley MacLane, actress

One of theweaknesses of our age is our apparent inability to distinguish our needs from our greeds.

—Don Robinson, writer

45.

A Short List

A short list of things you can do happily without that may surprise you:

- marriage
- kids
- sex
- close friendship
- romantic love
- an abundance of money
- youth.

My contention is that anyone, regardless of temperament or upbringing, can live temporarily or permanently without any of the above—and enjoy life immensely. At the same time I'll just reiterate that *if you can be sure that the circumstances are very favorable,* that is if they can be found in their higher levels as illustrated in this book, each one of these states is a tried and true path to some measure of solid happiness.

It's about time to take a closer look at a fatal member of the above list.

Part 3: Making the Single Life a Good Thing

Lovers are fools, but Nature makes them so.

—Elbert Hubbard, writer

To be in love is merely to be in a state of perceptual anesthesia—to mistake an ordinary young man for a Greek god or an ordinary young woman for a goddess.

—H.L. Mencken, writer

46.

Looking Calmly at Romantic Love

※

Romantic love is the grand dream of life, realized beautifully by a few, tasted by some, glimpsed by others, a tenaciously acted unfelt role for the majority. The anticipation of it causes the heart to flutter from adolescence, and in some is still capable of transforming that organ into a butterfly very late in life. That's the key, you know, the flutter. Romantic love alone, really, is capable of producing a wild flutter. Having the cockles of your heart warmed is as cold as death compared to the romantic love-flutter. But, thrilling though this may be, it will not last in its full glory even if love persists, and it is really no more than an internal sparkler: a brilliant but brief lighting-up of your life. Remove the love-flutter and there may still be much sustenance left in this love if it's substantial, but what makes it appear so magically precious is gone and it becomes possible to make a somewhat dispassionate review of its merits.

And as is made plain by the high divorce rates, cases of spousal abuse mutilation and murder, and all the long-suffering couples who for some reason put up with each other though you can cut the resentment between them with a knife, more careful review of merits is generally called for.

You need to do whatever it takes to mute the love-flutter for a hard objective look at both the loved object and romantic love itself. Starting with romantic love, you might ask yourself such questions as:

- Am I prepared for a series of emotional tempests of various degrees?

- Can I recover from them quickly and completely?

Part 3: Making the Single Life a Good Thing

- Is it a good idea to spend, in my current circumstances, large amounts of time building a relationship?

- Do I want, again at the present time, to allow someone to attain the right to become fiercely emotional about certain decisions of mine?

47.

My Qualifications for Writing this Book

✶

In his book *The Pursuit of Happiness* social psychologist David G. Myers has a section dealing with marriage and its effect on well-being. In it he states "In the United States ... fewer than 25 percent of unmarried adults but nearly 40 percent of married adults report being 'very happy.'" He gives as one of the reasons for this that "married people are more likely to enjoy an enduring, supportive, intimate relationship, and less likely to suffer loneliness." All this may very well be true. And yet this has not been the truth of my own life. I have experienced more than one long-lived love relationship that, though not marriages, combined all the positive qualities you could desire, as well as experienced lengthy periods of living almost entirely unattached. I honestly cannot say which were the happier times: starting, that is, from the time I emerged from my post-first-love funk until today, more than ten years later.

This is both my primary reason and primary qualification for writing this book: I have been very happy on my own. Instead of being based primarily on statistical studies of other peoples' confessions as to if, when, how much, or how little, they experience happiness, this book reports such information secondarily as a complement to and an alternative to my own detailed recipes for single happiness, based on my personal happiness when single. Because I have not endured being single, I have thrived in the single life, both in and out of relationships, and I *know* you can too. I *know* the raw materials exists for you to make it a good thing.

In the next two Parts we will explore these raw materials and discover ways to fashion them and fit them and juggle them so as to transform the potential of the single life into thriving reality.

Part 3: Making the Single Life a Good Thing

What a commentary on our civilization, when being alone is considered suspect; when one has to apologize for it, make excuses, hide the fact that one practices it—like a secret vice!

—Anne Morrow Lindbergh, writer

A man is an accessory, like a pair of earrings. It may finish the outfit, but you don't really need it to keep you warm.

—Rosemary Mittlemark

Part 4

Thriving in the Single Life (Among People)

※

Part 4: Thriving in the Single Life (Among People)

48.

Why it is Not Just Desirable—but Important—to be Happy Between Relationships

※

I don't think many young people see how pivotal happiness is in your life. I know I didn't. On top of this they only view it as achievable in a fullness approaching perfection in a middle stage of adulthood. And, as the crowning error, they have only one vision of the parts and circumstances which will account for it. This vision—loving spouse, good kids, good jobs providing a good income—must be sought *through* happiness, not *as* happiness. In other words I think the traditional way of questing for happiness is the reverse of what it must be to have any chance of realizing this universal vision of family bliss. Also I think there is no reason to place all of your chips for fulfillment in life on just one slot in the roulette wheel: marriage and children are not the only possible way to a rewarding life. In fact they are a good way to make a large part of life less than rewarding if they are seized on hastily to escape single unhappiness.

Even for people who are involved in a good relationship it is vitally important to be happy when not with their partner. The reasons why are essentially the same as those which demand a single person be happy. Therefore I will discuss both situations simultaneously for the rest of this chapter.

The practical importance of happiness throughout adult life cannot be overstated. It touches:

- professional and financial success;
- the types of people you have relationships with and the way you treat these partners as well as the way they treat you;

Part 4: Thriving in the Single Life (Among People)

- the types of people you have friendships with;
- physical and mental health.

All of these things will work on far less than optimal levels without consistent *daily* happiness. Even before you reach legal adulthood. Even as a person is completing their tender teens, if she or he does not have a sense of immediate happiness *based on some feature of their own person*, they may soon find themselves caught up in a whirlpool of events they would like to escape but can't. If she or he is miserable the chances are good a hasty marriage or a hasty career will be the result.

And in this one area people hardly change in a lifetime. Despite growing more savvy in business, more aware of the nitty-gritty requirements for month to month financial survival, people always remain as vulnerable as a child to bad treatment by others *if* they have no independent happiness. This ability requires a person to become a kind of happiness artist. And when I say artist I mean a person must learn to relish many of the things which make up a real artist's life-style and drive and fuel their creativity. But I'm not saying you should go buy paints canvases and an easel, or slabs of marble and a chisel.

Artist's generally love nothing more than to be by themselves. Of course they are not people haters, and many undoubtedly love to be with certain people *as much* as they love to be alone. Loving—not just being able to stand it—to be by yourself is the definition of independent happiness. Now what could it be that makes this attitude toward non-social life possible for the vast majority of an entire professional field? Part of it, certainly, has to do with the opportunities to indulge their creative impulses which being alone gives them. But this cannot account for it all or even most of it. The habit, it seems to me:

- of looking into yourself;
- of asking the imagination to let itself go while you record, or at least mark, the results;
- of absorbing more information and knowledge to be used in making more and better art;
- of simply thinking about everyone and everything without

interruption; must be a large part of the substance of their solo enjoyment. These activities, however, have nothing to do with artistic inspiration: they are what anybody, introvert or extrovert wealthy or struggling, can do if they make the effort to acquire the habit.

The result, as the Russian-born poet Joseph Brodsky wrote, is that we are taught "...the privateness of the human condition... it fosters in a man, knowingly or unwittingly, a sense of his uniqueness, of individuality, of separateness—thus turning him from a social animal into an autonomous 'I'." A key realization for everyone to experience in regard to sustaining happiness in any circumstances is that of the "privateness of the human condition." Inevitable, continual, multi-layered—these are words Brodsky might have placed before "privateness" if he had been in a mood to throw around adjectives.

As Social as we humans want to be, and many of us spend much of our time set in the midst of a social unit, we are at one level permanently alone; at another we are alone most of the time; at yet another about half the time. The world of thought, to take the first level, is not something in which other people can share. That is, the precise fluidity of a thought, with all its collage of associations, cannot be begun to be captured by speech; or words for that matter, which are only generic symbols for our individual feelings about the world to begin with. So that nobody can reveal their true, completely unique inner being to anybody—only the tip of its iceberg. This isolates most of the deeper perceptions, feelings, and so on from direct expression to anyone but ourselves. Possibly we can express some of them indirectly through art.

The second level, talking, is not only the primary way we communicate with other people, it is also an essential component of any dynamic, sustained exchange between people who are in love. Without it, being together quickly becomes a form of genuine isolation, in spite of all the best efforts of nearness: touching, kissing, gazing into each other's eyes, and—yes—even passionate love-making. Neither can this essential wire in the connection maintain its part in the hookup long

Part 4: Thriving in the Single Life (Among People)

without regular charges of meaningful dialogue.

And yet how much meaningful dialogue—that is, talk where both people utter mid-sized sentences—can even the best matched couple come up with every day? Even when they are in the early stages of getting to know each other, with truckloads of new personal history character and opinions to relate—not enough to fill half the time they are together. The rest of the time is filled with a word here and there in the midst of silence. Blessed silence, is how it is viewed almost without exception, when the conversation has been rich and steady.

Nonetheless, even in a day of togetherness such as described above, the people involved spend a large percentage of it left to their *private* thoughts, left to the single life. How much better is it to have the artist's or philosopher's plan at such times to resort to, of active thinking about the *nature* of things, including yourself, (excellently aided by books like this one by the way!) than the opposite! What is the opposite?

The opposite is what a person can't avoid when she or he doesn't take an active—I am tempted to say aggressive—role in sorting out and creating their thinking. And that is the miserably familiar-to-everyone circle of worries capable of extending its clammy touch to even the rosiest areas of your life. The more you indulge thought, letting it go where it will, the more you are gnawed by the teeth of greenback-riding dead presidents; money anxiety assumes outrageous proportions even for the most robust earners. Not to mention the rest of the long chorus line of fears all too ready to high kick it back onto center stage.

In short, when a catastrophe isn't looming around every corner, you wish one would because you're so anxious and bored; and all the while, a thin faint trumpeting in the background, the self-suggestion that the point in living is getting harder to see by the minute.

"The privateness of human life" at every level is of course substantially more private for someone not in a relationship. And yet the third and final level of the private life is only less private in a superficial physical way for the married. This level consists of the time we spend in bed waiting to fall asleep, sleeping, and getting up in the middle of the

Happy Between Relationships

night to visit the bathroom. Even if you are with people in a physical sense all day and much of the night, there is no way to pretend you are still pooling your consciousness with anyone once drowsiness kicks in.

You are in a private world, even if snuggling against someone in bed. Your mind is slowly marching down corridors of memory, approaching ever nearer a courtyard where Sleep's firing squad is checking and loading the weapons that will kill your consciousness. And just as in the case of facing a real firing squad, these last moments before you fall asleep can help put you face to face with raw, hard, cold realities. With the person who is really about to die, the usual sinking in of the finality, never seeing certain people and places again, etc. With the soon-to-be sleeper there is finality (that of the end of another day) but much more so there is a demonstration, a kind of slide show, of your independence from all the people currently in your life.

No matter how unbreakable you think your tie to them is when you are wide-awake, picture after picture insists otherwise. Relationship after relationship display their highlights and lowlights in scenes felt at the time to be relivable indefinitely, to your comfort or sorrow. Your father and mother's interactions with their child, your friends as a teenager confiding there problems and aspirations to you, lovers' beauty and passion—all of these people are either gone from your life or gone as you knew them.

But in the morning we get up from sleep and enter a world of waking dreams. "Hope springs eternal in the human heart," as the popular saying goes. Yes, but when it comes to hoping all your key relationships will remain, and remain unchanged to boot, a variation of the saying is equally true: "disappointment springs eternal from the human heart."

If,
- instead of believing in the improbable—that your current or some future relationship will last forever...

if,
- instead of dreading time alone and ignoring the unavoidable

Part 4: Thriving in the Single Life (Among People)

levels of privateness in human life...

If we can turn inward to not only face but *embrace* these conditions, turning loneliness into a pleasant and productive solitude, and the end of a relationship into the beginning of an adventure both in our inner as well as the outer world...

Then we will have achieved the artist's life-style and will indeed be artists even if we never decorated a canvas: painters, sculptors, writers, designers, discoverers of our own lives.

Come with me on an adventure, as we explore the possibilities of how this might be brought about.

And the spark as well as the sparkle, and the cure of all the mood-diseases, of an artist of her or his own life is their sense of humor.

49.

Developing Your Sense of Humor

I have always lived for humor. There are numerous studies that show that a sense of humor, laughing, laughing at yourself, promote health by lowering stress and exercising the lungs and cardiovascular system. So if you can laugh it is likely you can live—look no further for proof than the life spans of George Burns, Bob Hope, and Milton Berle. "And yet what is the point of living a long time if you haven't got anyone—or even anything—to live for?" Well, as I say, I have always lived for humor; that is, I live for being tickled, essentially. A frivolous and weird attitude, you say? Maybe. Of course humor is not the only thing I live for. However if I had to choose to give up all but one of the following biggies—love, sex, companionship, the ability to walk, humor—humor would be the one I would preserve. I even feel that it is sufficient to provide happiness by itself (provided, as always, that you are sufficiently fed and sheltered). And I strongly believe that it is accessible to anyone who is not in the middle of a traumatic event, that having a vigorous sense of humor is the most joyous of all conditions of life, and that its absence or rare occurrence reduces a person to a near-machine with, even in the best circumstances, a happiness more in theory than reality. In other words, I think humor is pretty important.

Before I get rolling, however, on the benefits of the humorous outlook on things and ways it might be cultivated, I want to address a few words to those who think absence of a grave reaction to 95 percent of possible occurrences is reprehensible frivolity. I agree that cracking a joke with a reference to somebody who has recently died is nasty. As in Dorothy Parker's irritated retort to a meddlesome woman who had asked her if she could do anything for her when her husband died: "Get me a new husband." And I admit that there are many jokes, not to mention

Part 4: Thriving in the Single Life (Among People)

off-color jokes, that are crassly inappropriate to almost all occasions. However the humorous outlook consists of a lot more than jokes; in fact many of its aspects need not have laughter as a consequence. A great example is irony.

With irony you are enabled to acknowledge and *feel* the unfortunateness, and even the tragedy, of events, while at the same time maintaining an abstract perspective which allows you to be aware of such things as the absurdity of the situation. For example, note the tragedy of Lost Cabin, as related by Bradford Angier in *How To Stay Alive In The Woods*. He tells of four turn-of-the-century gold miners who, their supplies running out, and not daring to undertake a journey through the snow to replenish them, died one by one. And yet "as I can substantiate from having camped there on several occasions, the vicinity abounds the year around with wild edibles." Now you can marvel in a highly amused way at the silliness of the situation, without in any way reducing your sympathy for the nightmarish end of the miners. What's more, by doing so you remember the story's lesson of the need for knowledge and ingenuity in a less fearful way—and it's always a good thing to keep fear, that nasty brute with its stress-like toxins, to a minimum in the system.

With the many forms of sophisticated humorous expression available—irony, understatement, satire, and so on—there is no reason that you cannot perceive and express, either just to yourself or aloud, a humorous side to most situations without being offensive, while at the same time cutting to the heart of the matter with all the sharpness of wit.

The pursuit of comedy is the pursuit of happiness. In order to show exactly what I mean by this, I must first propose a working definition of happiness. I think most people would agree that a pretty solid base for happiness would be, in mixtures varying from person to person: longer and shorter surges of interest excitement and fun capable of being counted on to occur daily in about the same total amount, interspersed with periods of quiet routine and even quieter semi-vegetation. Well then laughing, smiling quietly to yourself, bright eyes, grinning uncontrollably, whispering and giggling with friends lovers and coworkers—these things would seem to be heading us in the right direction!

Happy Between Relationships

Fun excitement interest and quiet—these are all by-products of the continual amusement brought about by a vigorous sense of humor. Fun is what the daily operations of life, such as preparing your dinner and even cleaning up afterwards, can become if you do it in the humorous spirit—chopping up vegetables to the tune or beat of the song on the radio, for instance. Excitement is the anticipation of being able to *keep yourself* entertained, through your ability to see the light side of most any situation, no matter what you end up doing. Interest is what you experience if what you are doing is mentally stimulating, as the pursuit of humor always is. Humor can be as intellectual a pursuit as any—it was not considered a waste of brain cells by some of the greatest intellects ever, like Shakespeare, Churchill, Joyce, and so on in a very long list. Quiet, true restful quiet, is what results after periods of amusement.

Of course it helps to have goals you are very serious about to plug your sense of humor into—which is a very mutually beneficial situation. Here humor is given much fodder in all the materials so earnestly considered, while the serious goal is continually having its burden lightened by the added fun excitement interest and quiet derived from keeping a humorous perspective.

But even if you currently have no goals in your life that you are passionately pursuing, whatever is in your life can be the source of enjoyment if only you choose to see from a humorous perspective. And it is mainly just a choice, although making that choice means that sometimes certain instinctive reactions will have to be identified and overridden by the lighthearted attitude inherent in the humorous outlook. An example of such a negative reaction would be if you were at the airport and were notified that the mild snowstorm forecast for your destination has been upgraded to a blizzard: a long delay, possibly overnight. If you have not trained yourself to take such major inconveniences in stride, it is likely this situation would cause something on the order of continual ranting and raving or, alternatively, continual moping until and beyond the end of the delay. If you have learned to see the humor in situations, and to laugh at yourself when appropriate, the stress-bomb of your initial annoyed reaction will be defused in a fizzle of self-laughter. This will lead you to find amusement in the

Part 4: Thriving in the Single Life (Among People)

pointless misery of your fellow delayed, which will lead you to help relieve and divert them and yourself with cheerful conversation.

But the choice of seeing from the humorous perspective must be followed by more specific reasoning than "This is a silly situation" or "That was ridiculous", you must make an effort to make somewhat clear to yourself why this is so. In the case of the airport delay, the likely reasons to be amused would come from thoughts like "Here everyone is sitting around looking angry and bored when they have stumbled upon an excellent opportunity to meet new people and socialize in a leisurely way." In this way you not only are penetrated more deeply by the richness of the humor and can communicate it to others, but you develop a key part of your philosophy of life.

If, however, you have a difficult time in seeing even a hint of humor in certain situations, or perhaps most situations, do not despair—there may be a simple solution. Social psychologists have found that actions influence attitudes. Clark University psychologist James Laird conducted an experiment on students to discover the effect of artificial frowning and smiling. The result: the phony smilers were made far more giggly by watching cartoons. So that instead of holding off until you are wholly convinced there is rich humor in a given situation, pretend somewhat and exaggerate the little you feel. Perhaps this will trigger a gradual insight into the depth of humor built in to most every situation involving human beings. This depth of humor exists because people:

- are too serious;
- take their troubles too seriously;
- forget that getting angry looks funny;
- are liable in the complexity of human affairs to make silly mistakes;
- tend to have at least a couple of quirky mannerisms of speech; gesture, and expression;
- are full of contradictory behaviors.

I don't think anyone would attempt to contradict me—except maybe

Happy Between Relationships

Scrooge before being reformed, afflicted with hemorrhoids and PMS to boot if that were possible—when I claim that people are humorous. Even people who rarely interrupt their frowning would admit (though maybe only after mild torture, like being persistently tickled) that they have at least once been forced to snicker at the behavior of a Homo sapien. But why is this? Why do we laugh and smile, why do we squint powerfully and turn red-faced with a rush of irresistible bubbly emotion, at the sight of a person being silly and not when we see waves crashing on the beach or trees bending in the wind? True, we do laugh at animals, but this is only because we identify human traits in them and think of them as funny-looking humans as they perform these traits. Understanding why people laugh or feel amusement through human behavior will make it possible to identify more humorous situations. And to derive a more hearty amusement through a sharper discernment of fine points and variations.

In the fifteenth edition of the *Encyclopedia Britannica* laughter is defined as a reflex, with no biological purpose other than to release tension. It is shown to be the result of aggressive malice discharged in the easiest most socially acceptable way. The malice may come from a belief in superiority over or lack of sympathy with the human source of the laughter. In fact the American psychologist William McDougall is quoted in the article as having believed that " laughter has been evolved in the human race as an antidote to sympathy, a protective reaction shielding us from the depressive influence of the shortcomings of our fellow men." However, the aggressive hard-hearted character of laughter is acknowledged to be softened somewhat in the subtler varieties of humor where "it may be so faint that only careful analysis will detect it..."

Once again, as with most of the ideas of eminent men, I tend to see a distinct possibility of truth in these theories—that mean and violent thoughts and emotions are the cause of laughter. Take practical jokes. Take dirty jokes. Take most any joke formula—they are all pretty clearly festering with sleazy little emotions. But I am not interested in jokes for my present purpose; I am not interested in make-believe people and situations or famous ones; I am interested in real people—that is, the ones in the same building with you, that you can see, and whose

Part 4: Thriving in the Single Life (Among People)

exhaled air is quite possibly mingling with your own. Laughing at these people, inwardly of course, is, or rather should be, a wholly different situation: one where your aggressive exhilaration is balanced by more personally and socially useful feelings.

This sort of laughing at other people is a great reaffirmation that people and their various behaviors are not to be feared (except in the very rare case of a violent person), not legitimate sources of nervousness, dread, and so on; they are just imperfect creatures like yourself, at some level of consciousness aware of this (if not all too aware), to be treated with the compassion and sensitivity that imperfect creatures like all of us are always thankful for. Realizing this, you don't openly laugh or make remarks or expressions that hint you are superior to whatever made you laugh. And let me just make it clear that laughter in the sense in which I am using it does not always or even most of the time imply laughing to scorn or even milder forms of disapproval of behavior. You might laugh to yourself at the way a grandmother spoils her toddler grandchild at the beach, constantly bringing the child new toys, not letting it go unentertained for a single moment—but at the same time you can admire the caring nature that leads to the absurd excess. You might find laughter in the infatuation of a young couple who become so oblivious to everything but themselves that they don't realize the waitress has been waiting to take their order for ten seconds—without jealous scorn, indeed from delight at this reminder of your own silly behavior when in love. And this kind of laughing at other people can bring another most precious gift: the ability to laugh at yourself.

It is important to be able to laugh at yourself. It is simply the speediest, most effective, and pleasantest way to restore your life—and human life for that matter—to the proper perspective. When you make a Freudian slip in conversation, walk out of the bathroom with toilet paper stuck to your shoe, have a bad hair day, don't get irritated or mad with yourself. This is the perfect opportunity to deflate any pretensions or other kinds of mental fat such as excess seriousness or gloominess by acknowledging, through laughter, the healthiness and strength to be had by not letting anything short of full-blown tragedy bother you. How much more practical is it to laugh at every mistake, misunderstanding, blunder that you make than to scold yourself and

Happy Between Relationships

dwell gloomily on these things! The former allows you to happily try again immediately. The latter increases general cautiousness while creating downright fear of the failed situations, which has to be painfully and gradually overcome to face them again.

Perhaps more important yet is the perspective on the big picture you can develop by learning to laugh at yourself. Laughing at yourself entails a degree of ridicule of man's pretensions as well as your own, a kind of razzing of humanity for believing that it is the end all and be all of this planet and most likely the universe. This is becoming humility, which opens the door to a variety of attractive attitudes which, again, not only can help you in your pursuit of independent happiness but also benefit others—animals and plants and any extra-terrestrial beings that may drop by included. By laughing at yourself you see that human beings are merely high-tech animals, whose vaunted mental technology, moreover, is truly an emerging technology, full of bugs compared to the sureness of the ancient instincts of animals. The consequent view of animals, as being more knowledgeable than us in the sense of deep instinctive wisdom, will surely make it harder to show them less respect than we do people. The same goes for trees and plants and any other forms of life that exist. People's faults, not just those of the people around you but the remotest foreigner's, you are much more likely to pity and empathize with than hate and inwardly curse when you are continually reminding yourself that you possess in your own brain the seed of every one of these follies.

But of course humor is not to be considered a panacea. Nor is it to be taken too seriously, as only a means for improvement of your mental and physical health, like a fun medicine that still has to be swallowed in painfully large pills. Humor is simply fun, in all its varieties from low to high, and the best way to use it is to look upon it as life and happiness itself. A laugh is a warm and nourishing helping of fat-free joy—a joy, unlike the joy of being in love, that is unmixed with doubt or fear and that instead of fading over time is ever renewed in its first freshness until the death of the mind does you part from humor.

Sharing humor can be an equally joyful experience. And it should be remembered that virtually every kind of humor is acceptable—provided

Part 4: Thriving in the Single Life (Among People)

it is in good taste and not done in order to vent spite or frustration. Puns, practical jokes, even some national or regional jokes, can be pulled off without anything to be ashamed of. Humor need not be brilliant or original to be worth it—I believe any attempt at all is appreciated by most people; it is an attempt to brighten the other person's mood as well as to renew their own amusement; and this is perceived as a special kindness, because the joke can give its owner renewed pleasure simply by thinking about it. It is just a matter of being sensitive to what might be offensive as well as other people's moods.

One of the best ways to cheer yourself up and get back into the humorous spirit and a generally positive outlook, is to read an amusingly written book. Better yet, take it with you when you go out and read a few lines every now and then. This will not only add smiles to your daily total but also disconnect you from any gnawing problems or worries, which is a huge relief and provides a refreshed eye with which to find solutions to the problems. I say 'amusingly written' because I don't mean this has to be a joke book or one filled with blatantly comic situations. An author that makes you smile usually provides a more engrossing stay with a better aftertaste than a joke teller who has been known to make readers spray their sodas in spasms of laughter. There is no quicker or surer way to overcome the blahs of gray weather, no more effective mental duster for when you feel coated with boredom, than to feed your brain a few lines written by someone who sees and delights in a great number of real and possible ironies and absurdities. It is an instant restorative to the balanced, healthy perspective—the humorous perspective on life.

The humorous perspective is essentially a very deep philosophical outlook on human beings and their civilizations, societies; on their struggles with the tendencies of their own nature as well as the tendencies of the world. This outlook can be used by anyone who decides to do so, with little or no clear understanding of it, by simply exerting their free will to laugh at instead of get mad at what smacks of absurdity. And yet, since the clearer our understanding of things is the closer we come to true sanity and peace, let me, for my own benefit as much as anyone else's, give some concise definition of what the humorous perspective on life is. The essence, I think, is the idea of balance. When

Happy Between Relationships

one of life's grim realities presents itself it is very easy to let the experience color many subsequent experiences. Soon you are reacting to everything that happens as a grim reality—even a picnic. If you live by the humorous perspective, on the other hand, when grim reality strikes—and I mean grim, such as losing a loved one or losing your job with a family to support—you don't despair. You are balanced enough to see, even through your trauma, the absurdity of any but a brief intense sadness in any situation. Believe it—the humor you had found previously in people and many situations they and you yourself had gotten into, makes it possible in a tragedy to put the most becoming face on the episode.

This is made possible because the person who lives by humor instead of an inflexible seriousness or a floating indifference observes more and thus thinks more. While the humorous person soaks up observations, the grimly serious person's observations are more like penetrations of his or her consciousness. She or he reacts to them as if being attacked—that is by keeping them to a minimum and lavishing negative emotion on anything rude enough to make itself noticed. The person ruled by apathy, of course, thinks very little of the very little she or he sees, and doesn't get riled up at every opportunity like the person ruled by gravity. However, they are siblings in that they are easily overwhelmed by forced major changes in their lives—it hits them like a thunderclap. By embracing opportunities to consider people, to see their humor and the beautiful fragile humanity behind it, you realize that people are essentially good but subject to error. Errors which include eating smoking and drinking too much, so that they sometimes die prematurely, also firing you when you don't deserve it or getting yourself fired by not providing what is required. When you see these tendencies every day it is never devastating to be hit by a major change, even the worst tragedies, for you are not only ready to grapple with the grief but also anxious to begin new experiences of the good in people—including yourself!

Part 4: Thriving in the Single Life (Among People)

Oh, the wild joys of living!

—Robert Browning, poet

Welcome, O life! I go to encounter for the millionth time the reality of experience...

—James Joyce, novelist

50.

Looking upon Your Life as an Adventure Novel

Perhaps it may be unrealistic to suppose that with the right job friends and attitude you could transform your days into frenetic plots. That you could experience globe-hopping rendezvous with danger and exotic dates (the danger easily overcome with your inexhaustible supply of lethal gadgets, the dates with your inexhaustible charm) like a series of James Bond movies. On the other hand, if that life sounds attractive to you why not at least try to live an aspect of it? If the world of James Bond is not appealing to you, why not seek some other adventurous life to aspire to or pursue adventure in some original way? For there are endless ways to be adventurous, in both large and small ways. Seems to me that, if there are scads of ways to live a life in an unbroken monotony, there must be just as many ways to break monotony into small pieces that would be far too tedious to glue back together. With a little effort it is quite possible to turn any life into a pretty good adventure novel.

The first thing to realize is that no place is unsuitable for an adventure. No place. No place is unsuitable for:

- intrigue
- fun
- laughter

as long as you have your imagination, or your imagination working with someone else's (say the author of a book). Places only *seem* dull and ordinary, because you've been to them before. The more times you've been to a place the more unthinkable it is that it is primed for an adventure. For example, your kitchen is not likely to be a place where

Part 4: Thriving in the Single Life (Among People)

you can feel it in the air that something of intense mystery and interest is about to materialize. And your lack of anticipation is, as far as the immediate surroundings are concerned, pretty well justified in this case. And yet, if you can visualize yourself in the broader scheme of things, not just working in your kitchen but in your kitchen in your house in your neighborhood in your hometown in your state and so on, all the current goings on that you know of and imagine in these places seem to whirl about your calm kitchen as if it were the eye of a hurricane. And so a sense of being caught up in an adventure is possible even in a place some would consider the precise opposite of the idea of adventure. And to show how easily attainable is the tingle of adventure, I will pause (not barefoot but with walking shoes poised to move on) in the kitchen. With only a dash of imagination, experimenting with foreign dishes and recipes can be more than just a new taste. It can be a direct experience of a different culture or country via the taste buds, setting off memories like fireworks if you've been to its place of origin, luscious flights of imagination if you haven't.

Moving on to less familiar and public places, adventure is to be found tirelessly lurking almost everywhere. In any of the places most people commonly go—supermarket, shops, restaurants, parks, movies—there is a very obvious yet almost always botched activity which, handled properly, is guaranteed to add a sense of intrigue to your day. I'm referring to watching people. How could someone watch people wrong? Well, for a start, many people don't watch other people at all; if they derive any pleasure from being in busy public places it is either on the subconscious level or from the use of people as a kind of 'warm' setting like you have on the stove. The liveliness around them is sensed more with an abstract mental eye than the two placed prominently at the front of the head.

Others, who have discovered that registering a few personal details here and there of passersby can spark something like interest, probably don't have any idea why they feel this near-interest. The result is that they, too, end up spending most of their public time submerged in their own skins. Their thoughts are mainly unrelated to where they are, merely feeling a commonplace, generic human presence flowing around them. And yet people wouldn't need a reason to find strangers interesting if

Happy Between Relationships

only strangers were a rare commodity. If that were the case, as it almost never is these days except in bleaker tundra areas of Alaska, then unfamiliar people would be to everyone the objects of excitement and mystery that they rightly are.

Here's why I think people-watching repays serious investigation. People are full of surprises. In order to feel they have a handle on an overwhelming situation, many people get into the fatal habit of pigeonholing everyone who forces himself or herself into their cramped consciousness: this one's a conservative businessman, that one's a neurotic housewife, oh no here comes a rebellious youth, a crusty old man, another aggressive bitchy career woman. It doesn't take long until people have become reduced to simple life forms hardly more interesting than an amoeba. Like Kentucky Fried Chicken, each individual that is registered does essentially one thing in life. If they display behavior that obviously doesn't fit, it is merely a glitch in their simple program. When you open yourself to receive a detailed impression of someone else, other people are transformed from dull types into jigsaw puzzles on the grand scale. Puzzles which would require a lifetime of intimacy to solve fully. And I mean any individual: the mistake of thinking some people are fascinating and others not is the sort of attitude that leads to ignoring as unworthy of attention people encountered casually or in passing. But the main thing, the joyous thing, is that the infallible individuality, the unpredictability, and the accessible depths of every person alive, make them can't miss prospects for entertainment learning and enjoyment purposes whoever they are and in whatever circumstances encountered.

Let's start with ways to farm passing strangers to reap a sense of having had an adventure merely walking down a busy sidewalk. Try to see past the obvious features of a person's wardrobe or the general look they are clearly trying to cultivate. Look for small but expressive personal touches, either consciously placed or the result of an eccentric omission, which are what really proclaim the personality. For example, take the hard-core cyberspace man. If you make the effort to look beyond the beard and mildly Bohemian hair length and glasses, you will no doubt find something, perhaps a glint of the outdoorsman in a wild corner of one eye, perhaps the confident curl of a sensual lip, or the

Part 4: Thriving in the Single Life (Among People)

glimpse afforded by an undone button of the mainmast of a naval tattoo—something to set off your imagination and abolish the stereotype.

When once you have become connected to someone in this way—by the strength of your stimulated imagination—you have as good as been plunged into the middle of a novel. It's up to you as to whether you wade back toward the shore of his birth or swim out further into the deep of his future. And this need not be a deliberate or prolonged action in order to capture that zing of being embarked on a mental journey. The zing, in other words, may be but a zap, consisting of no more than an encapsulating image or association. For example: a fat man with very straight black hair and a smallish moustache might strike me as a son of Hitler, and I might receive an image of a baby in a cradle with a little moustache giving the famous salute to his father. A woman's subtle smile might remind me of a woman seated at a table in a restaurant in an old movie, and I might wonder if that was her with dyed hair and a few extra pounds. In this way you can walk down the street taking shot after shot of a free liquor that won't leave a hangover even if you drink it all day and night.

Now let's explore adventures with people on a deeper but non-romantic level.

51.

The Benefits and Drawbacks of Friendship

A good friend has been the subject of much praise over the millennium. And I don't think anyone would deny that a close friendship is a valuable asset, something worth having and going to some lengths of effort and even expense to maintain. But what exactly is a good friend? Does the term imply faithfulness, standing by you in your times of trouble? Benjamin Franklin asserted that two-thirds of the only faithful friends a man could have were not human: "an old dog and ready money." And yet maybe he was only kidding, or half kidding. Let's look to a sage who sounds quite serious in his or her pronouncement. Ralph Waldo Emerson felt: "A friend is one before whom I may think aloud." We will take that under consideration. How often is one likely to find one before whom one may think aloud? Historian Henry Adams suggested that "One friend in a lifetime is much; two are many; three are hardly possible." Can friends be anything but a source of happiness, a source of joy? According to Warren G. Harding the answer is apparently yes: "My God, this is a hell of a job. I have no trouble with my enemies. I can take care of my enemies all right. But my damn friends, my goddamn friends. They're the ones that keep me walking the floor nights."

How does all this relate to the subject of this book? Should friends be sought more energetically when you are between relationships? Should friends be relied upon to fill a big part of the gap left by the ending of a relationship? Should they be eliminated or kept to a minimum, as Warren G. Harding might council? To make it possible to answer some of these questions, I will first take a look at the likely results of various degrees of involvement of a friend in the life of a single person, without regard to the quality of the friendship or the personality of the friend. Then I will consider the compensations of particularly close

Part 4: Thriving in the Single Life (Among People)

friendships—for everyone, but especially, of course, singles.

First the use of friends as a safety net when the trapeze act of a relationship falls out of sync and you find yourself falling. I suppose in the case of persons with a history of suicide attempts a support group of one kind or another is a matter of life and death—and one made up of friends is certainly preferable to one made up of attendants and doctors. There are benefits for someone without suicidal tendencies as well. You can learn who your real friends are (at least your most patient) and become more strongly bonded (if rather dependent) with this or these friends. Nevertheless, it seems to me that there are serious drawbacks to letting yourself be nursed by friends. It is like hibernating through the winter: you sleep cozily tucked away as the blizzards harmlessly beat the walls of your hideaway. One day you emerge to a spring whose thaw signals but the beginning of a spiritual winter, which you cannot escape except by ever-lasting hibernation.

Surrounding yourself with friends puts off your facing the situation, thrashing out your emotions, coming to conclusions, and finally moving happily off into the next phase of your life with a clean slate. Sure, you may have a friend who is willing to listen to you talk about your relationship; but this is mostly just complaining about your ex. It doesn't allow the truthful dialogue which shows faults on both sides such as is possible when you discuss a relationship deeply with your own conscience. There are of course the restless nights that are due to thoughts about your relationship, but these are not the product of a balanced analysis of the relationship; they are merely wild self-accusations springing from being tired and the darkness. It may be that the best way of recovering from the end of a relationship is to take a period by yourself, in which to face your conscience as well as the rest of your brain, receive its verdict and move on with your life without delay. (What might be done in this period as an aid to recovery has been discussed in Part 1.)

Once the initial trauma of facing the end of a relationship, and the struggle of coming to terms with it is past, then what role do friends play? To the person who is happily recovered from the end of being involved with someone for a substantial period, having friends can be

Happy Between Relationships

a boon for several reasons.

They provide flesh and blood companionship. There are many ways to enjoy people, both deeply and superficially, without making a single personal interchange with them. These ways are discussed throughout the book. All of them can be very valuable and some, like reading books, I consider essential to a true happiness. However, although happiness can be handsomely achieved without close friendships, there is a special jolt to be had from the personal exchange with depth. For the romantically unattached, this is your constant reminder of:

1) the joys of intimacy;
2) of the great value of not only being interested in someone but caring about them;
3) of not only caring about them but being intoxicated by their physical presence:

- the light in their eyes sparked by what you just said;
- the emotional musical instrument played through tones of voice;
- even the plain unadorned breath of their body, which is vibrant with warm exciting human life.

These are merely some of the flesh and blood enchantments of a close friendship, and yet without them one may begin to forget how wonderfully worthwhile a good romantic match can be.

Having close friends makes it easier to be without a relationship, making it more likely you will wait for a right person before you get back into a relationship. If a friend is regularly available for going places when you have the urge to go places not by yourself; if this friend listens and talks in amounts that seem reasonable to you; usually pays their share of the expenses; then, whatever else their person consists of in the way of personality, as long as it's not too demented, may well be worth exposing yourself to. This outlet is quite valuable apart from the relish you have for the details of the other's personality. It can help keep you from seeking a romantic commitment merely to fill your need to fill

Part 4: Thriving in the Single Life (Among People)

your passenger seat.

When you add a dynamic personality to the character of this hypothetical friend, one that you harmonize well with, then the practical value of the friendship takes on new dimensions. It is quite possible for a best friend to assume the character of soul mate. It is quite possible for a best friend to provide the near fulfillment of the deepest spiritual and emotional needs one normally thinks of as only capable of being reached through a matrimonial union. Indeed, why soul mates should be looked for more through marriage than friendship is pretty well beyond me. It is a very rare phenomenon in any case, and it seems that the chances of finding someone that understands and mirrors your soul are somewhat improved where sex is not an issue.

Sex and romantic love, while being a supreme experience when the minds stimulate each other before and after the bodies have done their act, is, when new, clouded with a poetic dreaminess. The love will survive the end of the dream if the minds have demonstrated they can click. Then, spiritual probing having overtaken physical probing, there is a chance that the couple will become the ultimate in soul mates. And yet this may be a year or several into a marriage, and it's a stake-it-all proposition. In the case of nonsexual friendship, there is no physical infatuation to cut through, little if any poetic hopes for its future. There is mostly practical appraisal of things like availability and reliability. The existence or non-existence of these basic facts is quickly established. Whereupon you move directly to a clear-sighted reckoning of the number of levels on which you click. This can be determined with quickness as well, and if it is only on the superficial level, it's all right and you try somebody else for a deeper connection—keeping the other person as a superficial friend if you like. There is nothing stopping you from auditioning, as it were, hundreds of people for the role of your personal soul mate in this way.

So what exactly is a soul mate, and why is it so valuable to have one around? If "a friend is someone before whom I can think aloud", then a soul mate is someone who is ever nearing the state of knowing your thoughts without them being spoken. If a friend is someone with whom you enjoy attending various events, a soul mate is someone you

Happy Between Relationships

consider—and who considers you—the event. If a close friend is like a sister or brother, a soul mate is like a twin sister or brother. The great benefit of such intimacy is the rare joy of knowing another person not only connects with your ways of thinking but has reacted to the world all along in much the same way as you have. And of course the sweet harmony of actually communicating with this person is a delectable feast, a rapid-fire exchange and development of ideas, which can be explored and moulded between you to a degree quite impossible unless two people are continually connecting. I need hardly stress how rare such real and consistent mutual understanding and identification is and how frustrating (what is common) a total lack of it can be.

Part 4: Thriving in the Single Life (Among People)

Friendship,n. A ship big enough to carry two in fair weather, but only one in foul.

—Ambrose Bierce, writer

I have no trouble with my enemies. But my goddam friends,...they are the ones that keep me walking the floor nights.

—Warren G. Harding, politician

52.

The Drawbacks of Friendship

※

While you are not likely to experience any substantial drawbacks in spending time with a friend who is a virtual soul mate, or even a good solid friend, yet some problems and irritations are inevitable in all friendships. In the case of exceptionally close friendships the benefits crush the drawbacks in every instance, however numerous its inconveniences. In the case of the majority of friendships, however, it seems reasonable that an ongoing debate with yourself should evaluate whether the friendship is truly worth the time it consumes in your life. The following is an analysis of ordinary friendships and what I see as some of their typical drawbacks. It also contains ideas about what might be done to remedy these defects.

Perhaps the primary drawback of ordinary friendships is that they tend to lead you into ruts of conventional behavior. You become locked into doing a certain activity or two with that person, which continue to be repeated long after enthusiasm for doing these things has been killed off by routine. These activities are not only repeated endlessly but seldom if ever are injected with the spice of variation or even any unusual or individual twist. You go to the same restaurant, the same bar, you watch the same programs on television together, see the same sort of movies, all the while chatting the same sort of chat on the usual everyday subjects. It's not necessarily that either of you have any individual lack of imagination or initiative, it's merely that the sparks you generate together never amount to much of a light show, are never capable of welding any real intimacy. The result is that you settle, through lack of inspiration, for doing what is conventionally done with friends and saying what is conventionally and politically correct.

Part 4: Thriving in the Single Life (Among People)

This stiffness in a friendship, once it has been established, is very difficult to alter and will likely lead to a number of what I am inclined to call negative consequences. Before listing some of these I want to stress that I think even a stiff friendship can be of value, especially regarding its service of providing flesh and blood companionship. The simple warmth of this human presence is often especially welcome to the person who has just recently determined to live for a time without a relationship.

Briefly here are some of the problems I see with the friendship which is less than a dynamic match. The whole set of drawbacks which come from this stiff conventionality I consider drawbacks primarily because much of the time spent in such a situation appears to me to be capable of being better spent. See if you don't agree with some of the items which follow:

- You have to smile and frown a lot when you don't really feel like smiling or frowning.
- You haunt certain haunts because, like certain ghosts, your enthusiasm for them died and you accept that you are doomed to haunt them.
- You find yourself discussing a familiar subject, which you only had a slight interest in the first time it was brought up.
- Worse still, you find yourself bringing it up.
- You find that food, and perhaps drinking or smoking or both, form the main activities instead of conversation—and you have a vague feeling of thankfulness for this.
- That falling in with large groups of people is a relief, kind of like coming in from the cold.

This as I say is largely due to conventional rather than natural reactions to the other person through a marginal rapport. Is there anything that can be done to improve the rapport? I think that there can always be improvement in any kind of relationship; especially in friendships of the same sex. In this particular kind of friendship, which I'll term an ordinary friendship, there may be a good chance of change for the better, especially if there has not been a persistent attempt at discussing personal

Happy Between Relationships

matters between you yet. Even if you do not understand or agree with the other's behavior or feelings thus revealed to you about their past, you will feel grateful for their trusting you and a degree of sympathy for their sufferings and gladness for their victories. And of course they will most likely grant you the same benefits for your own bold and noble openness.

And yet do not expect too much from this achievement of intimacy with someone with whom you click the way two toy monkeys with cymbals standing face to face do: artificially superficially and without harmony. You may come to feel some warmth of affection for this friend, and nonetheless fall back into a pretty empty routine with only a slightly improved rapport. The problem is that you probably became friends based heavily on being about the same age, body type, currently having a similar job or situation in life, moving in the same social circle, and so on. There was never any strong mental connection to take root in each others' brains and branch out in complex bonds of true affection interest and concern for the other person.

But there are at least two people in *everybody's* life who have the potential for this connection with them.

Part 4: Thriving in the Single Life (Among People)

There's nothing so sad as a 55-year-old orphan.

—Ella Grasso, politician

There are no illegitimate children—only illegitimate parents.

—Leon R. Yankwich, Judge

53.

Developing (or repairing) Your Relationship with Your Parents

If it is anything short of ridiculously impractical or impossible, one of the best investments you could make of your new-found time between relationships is in your parents. There is nobody who feels they have spent enough time with their parents, talked and confided deep feelings enough with their parents—when they are no longer alive. (The same of course goes for brothers and sisters; and if your parents are no longer alive apply the following to your siblings.) Even people who are good friends with their parents and see them on a regular basis are not without regrets when they die that they didn't have more joyful times together. For couples who are raising a family, establishing a home, working feverishly to pay for it and the needs of the growing family members, and in spare moments trying to fan the dwindling flame of romance or just renew enjoyment of each others' company, even giving a thought to their parents is an achievement, while a phone call is a kind of labor of Hercules. However, even people in this situation might find the time to contribute something substantial to their relationship with their parents, even if it is only a brief thoughtful letter.

What about parents who were not good parents, and those who were terrible cruel parents? Surely they don't deserve their children's efforts as adults to improve the relationship? In the latter case I believe this is true. If there has been extreme abuse, either physical or mental, such as molestation, severe beatings, constant put-downs, threats, an unnecessary neglect of material needs, such as food and clothing, then the parents in question should be thankful if you don't take revenge. They have no right to expect any degree of forgiving and forgetting on their child's part. What's more, if the grown child says to herself: "This

Part 4: Thriving in the Single Life (Among People)

is my mother and father and I can't hate my own parents. Besides they did the best they could, everyone makes mistakes and has faults. And anyway they did some good things..." the result is likely to be just more abuse. There is no reason to think the abusive parent or parents will change an attitude toward you that was strengthened by regular attacks over a period of years.

On the other hand, if the parents were not ideal, had their weaknesses like alcoholism or depression or incompetence in a certain job, and consequently failed to provide the proper emotional or material support for a time, you may want to consider forgiving them. Their abuse was not calculated, not mean-spirited—that is if in their frustration or despondency they did not go too far in taking out their problems on you. Spankings or slaps, some halfhearted curses or threats made in times of despair or extreme pressure, are not acceptable behavior and do not occur more than once or twice with good parents; and yet they may (not without considerable effort, of course) be largely forgiven by a generous person. And in many of these cases I think it may be a great benefit to both parties. Because these abuses arose from extreme states of mind, overriding good patterns of treatment. These external causes of abuse being removed in later life, there is a good chance these parents may be largely benevolent to you at this point.

And when less-than-criminal parents and their adult child can manage to classify the negative aspects of their past relations as flare-ups and frictions of minor, though regrettable, importance, then it becomes possible for a fascinating relationship to develop. It has the potential to be no less than a new relationship, and yet one with a past and a strange past at that. The old times seem like a former life. You were two or rather a series of different people. Constantly changing in appearance and your methods of interaction, there was one peculiarly fixed aspect— one had massive authority over the other. Now here you are, two adults of virtually equal height and vocabulary, neither with anything that could be called authority over the other, shaking hands. The next step may as well be to say "Dr. Livingston, I presume?" as anything else, because you have come to this point after the epic crossing of the dark continent of childhood and parenthood. Here is the source and beginning of an opportunity for an equally rewarding and epic exploration: each

Happy Between Relationships

others' minds.

The person who is between relationships is in an ideal position to embark seriously on this exploration. And the results of making this effort are likely to be beyond your expectations even after reading this. As you talk with a parent, asking questions about what he or she really thinks about things and why, it becomes increasingly clear that this person is a lot more like a slight variation on yourself than an authority figure.

You will come to see that they behaved the way they did as you were growing up because of what they experienced as much as who they were born. Specifically the way their own parents treated them shaped their reactions to being a parent. This is a highly valuable lesson to receive, and you receive it so it sinks in when a parent describes in vivid detail a few incidents in illustration. Secure in the knowledge that your parent was not simply being cruel to be kind when doing similar things to you—-just being a robot obeying its program to do this—you may be able to avoid passing this destructive habit on to your children.

But just as important is the knowledge you gather in these talks of your mother or father as a personality: to see as exactly as possible who they were and are and what they wanted and want to be. There is a saying that when a person dies it is like a library has burned down. In the case of your parents, it is a situation where you lose several of the most precious shelves of your own library in their fire. Their autobiography, a twenty volume or more work of relentless value and interest to you, contains in these thousands of mental pages an abundance of clues as to your own talents and tendencies, both to the good and the bad. In other words, in order for you to understand yourself thoroughly you must become a thorough biographer of your parents, adding their mental autobiography to your own. You must become a thorough:

- researcher of your parents;
- interviewer of your parents;
- analyser of your parents.

Part 4: Thriving in the Single Life (Among People)

Their life is a distorted reflection of your own, and in spite of the distortion the clearest mirror in which to see yourself.

However, from sheer love's sake, and also delight in a personality so fascinating in that it is elusively like yours at one moment and unlike the next, there is equal reason to talk deeply with a parent. Besides, the old adage is wrong: you'll be continually surprised by the new tricks these (excuse the expression) old dogs come up with. These tricks including insights and observations that people who are twenty years younger simply don't have a broad enough spectrum of experience to see by themselves.

Here are some subjects you might want to delve into with either of your parents:

- Their early love affairs, if not with your other parent.
- Their romance with your other parent.
- Their professional dreams.
- What they consider their major mistakes in life.
- Their opinions on general subjects, such as life, love, adventure, sex, celibacy, the city, the country—anything and everything.

This last one—asking their general opinions on various familiar subjects—may seem somewhat pointless. You know how they feel on most of these subjects already, right? Maybe, but do you know what they *think* on them? If they haven't expressed an opinion in plain words on a subject, your idea of their thoughts on it is likely to be off the mark at least in detail and quite possibly in substance. Because how a person ends up behaving in regard to a given subject is not always a good measure of their mind's verdict and deeply held beliefs on that subject. Nor are scraps of commentary they may have made on the subject, thrown out in moments of emotion or in a mixture with one of the many forms of humor.

For example, a parent may have much more open-minded views on love and marriage and sex than you always thought; the seemingly

Happy Between Relationships

inflexible traditionalism you may have perceived as their position on these issues may have been more a desire to ensure your not getting involved in complications, such as an early pregnancy, than, for example, a condemning of unmarried sex. So you may find that a parent who always seemed somewhat prudish towards sex is all in favor of unmarried sex between adults, possibly even early on in the dating, and who feels that living together is a legitimate alternative to marriage. Be prepared to make both major and minor revisions to your old mental notes and reports on these people. In fact you may find these documents thoroughly distorted or obsolete in the face of this deeper information. You may trash them completely and start new ones—more deep-seeing and scholarly notes, capable of doing justice to this central character in your personal family epic.

Continuing the adventure theme, let's now take a look at the intriguing adventurous aspects of the workplace.

Part 4: Thriving in the Single Life (Among People)

But it is not hard work which is dreary; it is superficial work that is always boring in the long run...

—Edith Hamilton, writer

Attempt the impossible in order to improve your work.

—Betty Davis, actress

Never allow your sense of self to become associated with your sense of job. If your job vanishes, your self doesn't.

—Gordon Van Sauter, writer

54.

Enjoying the Act of Work More Than the Money

Work, including projects and goals, needs to be enjoyed for itself at least as much as for the money it provides or may provide, and ideally should be enjoyed more than the money. If it is not then, inevitably with experience, the gleam of the cash-dazzled eye will flicker when it begins to sense the upcoming 'grind for the green' necessary to get the next payoff. On the other hand, if the work is interesting itself then, aside from feelings of minor guilt for being paid to have fun, your day becomes something to look forward to; every day becomes Sunday.

It does not take a powerful position in a company or creative or even unusual work to find your occupation interesting. Because if you do not *find* it interesting at first you may have the power to *make* it interesting. Because you have the power to:

- think of ways to innovate, that is come up with ways to make something easier or more challenging or put a personal stamp on it;

- interact with people you come in contact with on the job in more entertaining or meaningful ways, say through joking with them or taking a deeper interest in their lives.

You may not have enough of these opportunities to satisfy you, in which case find another job—at least, having made every effort, you will know for sure that the job is not for you. Say, for instance, you worked at a snack bar taking orders and working the register. Now, in itself, in all that strictly makes up the work, there is virtually nothing that could contain a spark of interest for anyone. It is just a monotonous grind of

Part 4: Thriving in the Single Life (Among People)

taking cash and making change and filling cups. And yet what is to stop you, if it is not very busy, from discussing the weather with your customers? Making jokes, asking opinions on current events, becoming friends with regulars and regularly exchanging news on personal affairs—what is to stop you from becoming an amateur psychologist, analyzing what these people tell you about themselves as you work, learning to detect patterns of behavior and their meanings .... What is to stop you from taking night classes and using this knowledge and interest to possibly get a degree in psychology?

The joy of work consists in the chance to apply your brain to challenging tasks which suit its temperament and to interact with people; only secondarily in making money, however much; not at all in having easily performed duties.

But, as we all know, there are distinct advantages to money.

55.

Saving Money: a Solid, Possibly too Obvious, Way to Increase Happiness When Not in a Relationship

※

Most people think of money as merely the means to acquiring a happy love life. It is merely the engine which propels your happiness, making it possible to date in high style, or get married buy a house and start a family. The mere acquisition of money by itself is not happiness. Well I don't agree with this. When you are without prospects in the love line or are presently not in the market for a love relationship, the unromantic fact that you are putting away money little by little should provide a form or aspect of happiness. Remember that happiness should not be defined narrowly and strictly, as one or two states of love in which everything is clicking along at near perfection; but freely paste that label on anything which provides a degree of steady internal warmth. Paste it on such non-romantic things as:

- good health;
- sufficient shelter;
- sufficient income;
- money saving;

and remind yourself daily that you have these things. Because if these things are not happiness itself, they are essential contributors, without which a full-blown happiness is not likely to occur. And of course the happiness produced by saving money need not be related only to the security it provides; it may be viewed in a future romantic role as enhancer of coming love relationships.

The best thing about this form of happiness is that very humble occurrences suffice to bring a renewed dose of it. For example, every

Part 4: Thriving in the Single Life (Among People)

time you save five or ten dollars by renting a movie instead of going to the theater, or go on a Sunday walk in the park instead of going to a football game, you receive a pleasant simmering happiness a lot like contentment. This comes from the feeling that you are doing something for your future instead of being manipulated by a greedy present. And I feel this is a particularly important attitude to cultivate: the future, even if you just turned ninety, should be looked upon as being just as important to live for as the present. In this there is the implication that middle *and* old age are as exciting as the prime of youth. And I will go further: it is quite possible for life to become more exciting the farther you get from the prime of youth. All it takes is an obsession with the development of mind, started as early as possible, with bodily pleasures and maintenance taking a still crucial but secondary role. Anyway, with this bright view of future possibilities, saving money by refusing to settle for any old relationship becomes a no brainer.

And so does making the best possible use of the time-gift you have when you find yourself in a state of independence. And at times you will find that, since you embraced your independence, being completely by yourself is just fine. Here's how to make it finer still.

Part 5

Thriving in the Single Life (in Splendid Solitude)

※

Part 5: Thriving in the Single Life (in Splendid Solitude)

56.

Using Media Contact as Relationship Substitutes

According to a study released June 24th 1997, loners get more colds. Of the 276 people involved in the experiment, 62 percent who had three or fewer relationships caught a cold; only 35 percent of those with six or more types of relationships caught colds. Whatever it is that causes this social immune boost, one thing seems clear, according to psychologist Sheldon Cohen: " Having many types of relationships was more important than the sheer number of people in their social networks." Now, this being the case, is the single person, who is automatically without the advantage of a partner and the partner's family and friends, doomed to be punished by their immune system? Is there no way to compensate for the absence of the shot in the arm received by the relationship-rich? Well I think there is—and I, a single, have not had a cold in several years.

The first and most common-sense way of maintaining your immune system as a first-class germ fighter is to take care of yourself. This is confirmed in the above-mentioned article, which notes that the highly social group "are motivated to take better care of themselves because their contacts promote feelings of self-worth, responsibility, control and meaning in life."

From this it would appear that those who are relationship-limited, whether by choice or force of circumstances, are doomed to a kind of lost-soul status. I mean when you're lacking in "self-worth, responsibility, control and meaning in life," it would seem that you should consider yourself lucky if you only have the blues. And I do not doubt that a number of loners and semi-loners are, if not completely miserable in the above categories, at least deficient in them. And by

Part 5: Thriving in the Single Life (in Splendid Solitude)

deficient I mean not on the level I believe they should be. For the reason I wrote this book is that I think singles, or anybody on their own for whatever reason, do not need to feel lonely or like losers or that any happiness or pleasure they might feel is in any way inferior to what people in good relationships feel. In other words I have set out to show that the lacking self-worth, meaning in life etc., is wholly the result of the cultural stereotype of 'how it should be'. Yes, the one that is pounded into our brains from the dawn of consciousness in fairy-tale TV and movie happily-ever-aftering couples and bad-guy loners.

Not to say that I think relationships can be ignored as a component of happiness. I strongly agree with Sheldon Cohen's conclusion about a diversity of relationships being important. Isn't this contradictory? No, because you can be a loner and still have an assortment of relationships. How's that? Let me explain.

What has worked for me has been a combination of two varieties of contact with people requiring a minimum of commitment. The first is an almost ideal kind of relationship when at its best, and this kind of contact might be called *media contact*. These sorts of relationships range from the interactive experiences possible on people's Web sites to the remote actual exchanges of words and thus ideas and experiences in letters and e-mail; from the faces of TV to the (larger) faces of the silver screen; from the rambling voices of talk radio to the music of CDs tapes and radio; from newspapers to Web sites to books. Some will object that these are not relationships but 'relationships' and that these are the sources, especially TV, of life-wasting that commonly make those on their own feel empty. This is of course true: they are not full-blooded interactions with others and they are responsible for massive amounts of emptiness—or at least go-nowhere escapism. However I believe this problem is through *misuse*. The objection that they are not relationships is granted—they are relationship substitutes and supplements.

As relationship substitutes and supplements, they are not to be relied on for filling all of your need of other people. They might take up the majority of your free time in such a way as not to waste a minute of your time—and yet leave you feeling empty if a substantial amount of

Happy Between Relationships

face to face, smile to smile, laugh to laugh, contact is not made with people. And yet, if used discriminatingly, an assortment of print and electronic media can form the equivalent of several highly informative, colorful, adventurous, and—even more rare and wonderful—highly obedient and totally undemanding friends. By discriminate I mean to find a good balance among whatever media you have access to and enjoy.

Now what is a good balance? To my mind this consists of using the various media to create a cocktail, which intoxicates without putting you to sleep, stimulating and relaxing, alternately so sometimes, simultaneously at others. And this is not a terribly difficult balance to achieve. It just takes determining how you can *use* these media to achieve goals major and minor—a sense of rich, progress-oriented happiness being fostered by all.

TV, for example, can actually be useful for more than an evening filler. Through selective watching you can learn a lot and, most likely, a lot about the subjects most useful to you in the area you wish to advance yourself in. And advancing yourself is the essence of happiness anytime—whether in a career or just building areas of expertise. An ordinary good friendship is one in which two people are helping each other advance themselves, if only in becoming a better expert on their own natures. The TV to be avoided at all costs is not a fixed list of programs or kinds of programs I or someone else finds unrewarding; it is watching—even the most well-done program—in a half-aware half-doze. It seems to me that if you're tired, taking a nap is a far-superior way to get rest than lolling in front of a flashing screen. Nonetheless, if lolling in front of a flashing screen does wonders for you, that's all right—as long as you can break away from that mode before too long and move on to something involving active pursuit of goals.

On the other hand, you may just want some nights to be with interesting people, *see* interesting and attractive people—and that's it. In other words you don't want particularly to go and find someone to talk to, you just want a quick people fix before getting on with a project. In this case it is a perfectly healthy expedient to go and rent a relationship-rich movie or watch a couple of TV sitcoms. This isn't escapism in any

Part 5: Thriving in the Single Life (in Splendid Solitude)

regrettable sense; it can be a contribution to well-being, and as nourishing an exposure to the unpredictable wonders of human behavior as most casual face to face encounters. It *can* be, that is if the writing is good and the characters are not stereotypes. And the key to this practice is to ensure that the movie or the show are *refreshing* by making them a break from your pursuit of knowledge.

The same goes for casual acquaintances. They can be a wonderful additional source of spiritual nourishment—if they are viewed as a break from chasing challenging goals and not as a major spiritual food group, as it were. For more on ways of getting the most out of casual relationships, see Part 4.

By using the various media and chance exchanges of conversation with people casually met, you get more than the equivalent of a few more individuals in your life: you get to keep as much personal freedom as possible. Because, as nice as it is to be mutually committed to a relationship with a romantic partner or close friend, you are in some measure sacrificing your freedom. A certain percentage of your actions become determined only partly by what you want to do: you go from the head of a sole proprietorship to just another committee member when with them or dealing with their needs or demands. You get an awful lot of this committee member feeling in both bad and good romantic relationships. It is a shame, it seems to me, to just substitute more of the same feeling by running to and submerging yourself in some other kind of committed relationship (like relatives, old friends, new friends you don't really like, etc.). One of the glories of being between relationships is the experience of rarely, if not never, feeling resistance from outside to any fancy that takes you. Again utilizing the media as relationship substitutes, as well as casual acquaintances, makes for a nice version of having your cake and eating it too.

57.

Making Happy Progress in Solitude

Once loneliness has begun to be conquered (through methods cited earlier in "Exterminating loneliness and boredom" in Part 3) and converted to solitude, a key to keeping loneliness from coming out of extinction is to put solitude in motion. "Human beings are all about movement," wrote Robert Louis Stevenson, and a sense of solitude and a sense of serenity are only rarely connected. The only reason they are associated at all is because these emotions are overwhelmingly felt at some point by anyone who has been to a national park—even if they tell themselves they are not nature lovers. Otherwise a serene solitude quickly becomes boredom. What is possible when solitude is put in motion boils down to what I will call self-productivity. Self-help books, for that matter, boil down to various forms of self-productivity.

Self-productivity means producing or bringing into the outer world your inner self; or adding to the arsenal of that inner self, to be brought out at some future time. It contrasts with the productivity required of you at the workplace in as far as you are the ultimate product being manufactured, whatever you create in the process. When it is realized that certain kinds of activities in solitude will add dimensions to yourself and your view of the world, any effort required seems worth it. And it may as well be called work. After all, any activity is a kind of work; exercise is commonly referred to as a *work*out, and in physics it means simply energy expended by natural phenomena. Beyond this, the image of work needs to be rehabilitated. Work is not something to be liberated from; the kind of work which allows for self-productivity is work that gives the opposite effect. Instead of wanting a few days off from this kind of work, you wish that the week contained *eight* days for doing your job. You wonder how anybody can just rest when such a paradise

Part 5: Thriving in the Single Life (in Splendid Solitude)
is available to them!

Here are some of the basic ways to become self-productive:

- Seizing every opportunity of improving your vocabulary.
- Seizing every opportunity to see something new.
- Seizing every opportunity of seeing familiar things in a new way.
- Seizing every opportunity of having a new experience.
- Seizing every opportunity of making an effort.
- Seizing every opportunity of increasing general knowledge.
- Seizing every opportunity of building a level of expertise in a specific area.
- Seizing every opportunity of getting beyond small talk with an acquaintance.
- Seizing every opportunity of thinking and expressing.
- Seizing every opportunity of planning and dreaming.

This may sound exhausting, and it is if you try to do all ten in a big way every day. Like if you tried driving great distances to find a place you haven't seen before every day. Attempted on a small scale, however, all ten things can be done on any given day—even after a tough workday. In fact they can make a tough workday a lot easier to bear if practiced during free moments and moments of semi-solitude at the workplace. And of course there are moments for doing such things as building your level of expertise, and seeing familiar things in a new way, in the midst of the work. However, as this section is about the uses of solitude, I will illustrate how this might be done in your free time. (See Part 2 "Continuing to be happy between relationships *in* your next relationship" and Part 4 "Enjoying the act of work more than the money" for ways to spice up the workday.)

Here's how in one relaxed evening you might easily accomplish all ten items of the above list. On arriving home after a busy workday, you change clothes and begin preparing dinner. Here you could take care of two of them by fixing an exotic new dish, which need not be very time consuming, and planning meanwhile how you could get the most out

Happy Between Relationships

of your evening. Eating dinner in front of the TV set, you could immediately check off two more by watching an unfamiliar program. This would allow you to see something new and increase your general knowledge at the same time. Finishing a leisurely dinner, going to your reading chair, you are in the vicinity of three more. Depending on the type of book you sit down with, if you have a dictionary you can make a few solid contributions to your vocabulary, make an effort to understand the author's ideas, then weigh and evaluate them. With a book on a topic you know something about, reading a few pages increases your level of expertise, improves your vocabulary, and allows for some invigorating thinking. If you write down one or two of these thoughts you will have covered self-expression. The effort involved in the reading thinking and expressing will be hardly noticed if the book interests you; nonetheless it will be a source of satisfaction to you. A few minutes of quietly looking about your bedroom before going to bed, gently making yourself see the normally blurry details of some part of the room, qualifies as seeing familiar things in a new way. And that covers all the uses of solitude for self-productivity in one commonplace, relaxing evening.

Being self-productive can be highly satisfying because its benefits can work on several levels. In one evening like the one described above, you can contribute substantially to:

- your social skills;
- your professional skills;
- your general understanding and wisdom.

As a result of this progress your self-esteem is boosted; as a result of the whole process, the interesting and challenging variety and its benefits, your happiness in solitude becomes delicious. You begin, in other words to live by the artist's mind-set. To convert your life into the art which makes this life precious to you regardless of the way other people treat you.

A few words as to how you can receive benefits on the levels I mentioned above:

Part 5: Thriving in the Single Life (in Splendid Solitude)

- Social benefits. The idea of improving social skills in private sounds like a contradiction in terms. Not necessarily. By itself it certainly won't give you that suave self-confidence in social situations, but there's no denying that a powerful vocabulary and an abundant fund of general knowledge are the stuff interesting talk is made of.

- Professional skills. You can watch a program or read a book with some real relevance to your job and still be entertained. For example a beautician could watch a program on art or history or just a movie set in the past, and perhaps learn more about the possibilities of hair arrangement and makeup. A chef or a baker could read a book by an author like Charles Dickens, who features magnificent descriptions of feasts, and possibly be stimulated to some new creation. But both the beautician and the chef would also have abundant and exciting diversion from the subject matter of their jobs: in the other elements of history or art for the one, in the great characters and story of the other.

- General understanding and wisdom. Every time an effort is made to learn something there is the chance of increasing your general understanding. Especially if you are aware of this. If when learning something you are aware of how the subjects of your study are related to other things, you are increasing your wisdom. For example, when you use the World Wide Web to find information about a place where you are thinking of going on a vacation, you can do a lot of learning on a wider level. If you are not very experienced in using a computer, the quest to find whether roads are open at the passes, the hotel rates and descriptions, and the local highlights and events—every step in the process may increase or reinforce general understanding. Even if you are something of a veteran on the Internet, there would still be a likelihood of making a side discovery of some kind. This could consist of an insight into human nature, such as a reinforcement about your opinion of webmasters: that they are by and large extremely generous with their knowledge most

Happy Between Relationships

likely. (Most webmasters, whether professional or not, go out of their way to provide links to other sites that may interest.) From this the wisdom might be drawn that people in general are helpful for the most part—in the right circumstances.

These characteristic behaviors of self-productivity must of course be steadily performed to make an impact on happiness. That is, they must become habits—habits that take the place of less useful ones.

Part 5: Thriving in the Single Life (in Splendid Solitude)

Nothing is stronger than habit.

—Ovid, poet

It is through contact with living nature that we are reminded of the non-mechanical aspects of all living organisms, including ourselves, and can sense the independence, the unpredictableness, and the mystery of the living as opposed to the mechanical.

—Joseph Wood Krutch, writer

58.

Cultivating Dynamic Habits

※

The pioneering psychologist William James called habit "the enormous flywheel of society, it's most precious conservative agent." Some, however, consider it less than precious, philosopher and author Miguel de Unamuno for one, who called it a "near neighbor to annihilation." My belief is that, taken all in all, habit can be a very positive force in the life of an individual, as well as in the life of the community as William James points out. It is quite clear to people that bad habits can lead to the most serious problems and even tragedies; drinking too much, everyone knows, leads to alcoholism, which leads to losing your job, which leads to spousal abuse and a smorgasbord of further nightmares.

So why does anybody drink at all if they know, as they do, that alcohol has the potential to turn their life into a nightmare? Because, taken in moderation, alcohol does little apparent harm, and provides a dose of pleasure relaxation and escape. The only thing is that, if circumstances become hard to handle, especially if it's worse than any previous experience of difficulties, then your harmless habit presents a natural solution. Your mind and body, obedient to the habit of a daily drink, will almost automatically put that drink, now a deadly temptation, in your hand—*even if you are conscious of the danger.* This tenacity of habit is what makes it a potentially powerful force for good. The key, of course, is to choose the right habits, and also to respect the power and repercussions of every habit that is formed—down to the smallest.

First it is important to establish a few good habits in dealing with habits. One that is particularly important is maintaining awareness of your habits. Establish in your consciousness a kind of supervisor of your habits. Like a watchtower guard in a prison complex, detached, coldly

Part 5: Thriving in the Single Life (in Splendid Solitude)

observant and analytical of the motions of the prisoners below, it should be ever ready to implement correction procedures. Then you will be protected from one of the main dangers of habit: takeover. Yes, just as prisoners sometimes dream of overthrowing the prison authorities and making a mass jailbreak, then to overrun the countryside and take hostages—so certain habits would like nothing better than to break their bounds and hold previously flourishing parts of your life as permanent hostages. The only difference is the inmates never realize their dream, habits often do. Left unmonitored, most any habit has the potential to begin a subtle expansion and become a monster before you realize it. I've already mentioned alcohol, here are some other common ones: food, shopping, work, sex, television, etc. All of these are, of course, good, healthy activities—ambitious ones, however, that dream of taking over and running wild.

Another good habit to impose habitually on your habits is that of varying routines slightly. By doing this you get simultaneously the benefits of habit (regularity, mental comfort, assurance that a procedure will work, and general coziness) and the benefits of creativity (mental stimulation, maintenance of the ability to change, freshness, development of cleverness, subtle thinking, and a feel for artistic living and the artistic touch in general). But just as important as the above benefits is the way these slight variations keep you from becoming wrapped up tight in layers of repeated identical routines. Because when this happens, though you may be well preserved by them, you are about as free to do new things and go new places as a dead mummy in a sarcophagus. And on the rare occasions when dead mummies do break free they find it very difficult to adjust to life (excuse me, death) outside the sarcophagus—just ask Boris Karloff.

And when I say 'slight' variation in routines I mean it. Healthy alterations in habits can consist in changes as seemingly inconsequential as getting up on the other side ('wrong side' is a myth invented by someone controlled by their habits) of the bed; adding a new expression, rhythm, gesture, etc., to your methods of personal communication; preparing a favorite dish in a new way, or even just using a new spice; putting the stamp on an envelope first instead of last; opening and knocking doors with your left hand instead of right; reversing a pair of

Happy Between Relationships

steps in a common work procedure, or even doing part of a crossword puzzle (especially if you never do these puzzles) before settling in to work habits. What is being done here is essentially training your habits to realize who is boss—the way a sled driver trains his or her dogs so that they don't end up setting the destinations, like their favorite trees. To use a loftier simile, habits, in order for you to receive their optimum benefits, should work like an automatic pilot: you switch it on for consistent performance and override it regularly whenever the challenge and excitement of a storm arises. And then, letting go of the controls and sinking back in a semi-dose in the pilot seat, hand it over again to "Auto" and wait until another opportunity for meaningful action arises.

Now for the acid test of habits: which contribute to happiness in extreme circumstances?

Part 5: Thriving in the Single Life (in Splendid Solitude)

Alone, alone, all, all alone,
Alone on a wide, wide sea.

—Samual Taylor Coleridge, poet

Be thine own palace or the world's thy jail.

—John Donne, poet

59.

Finding Happiness when in Forced Isolation from the Usual Social Scene

※

There is no point in my trying to deny that isolation from the opposite sex is a difficult thing to deal with for any heterosexual person. When a person in the Navy or other professional sailor must leave his or her family or relationship for a period of months, there is no replacing the particular kind of warmth of that intimacy. It's much the same for a sailor without anyone awaiting their return; he or she also finds the prospect of little if any possibility of intimate interaction (either talking or touching) with the opposite sex hard to face. Again this cannot be replaced, it is a vacuum in the chest. And yet I think it is possible to contain this emptiness in the heart to an isolated place of its own, by filling the other parts of the heart with seeds and watching them sprout.

People spending prolonged stretches of time at sea are, of course, not the only ones who suffer from this kind of isolation. They come from diverse professions, ranging from the already-mentioned sailor to the professional athlete; from rock stars to field geologists to traveling salespeople to people in the other branches of the military. However I would like to take the person isolated at sea because it is probably the most extreme case of forced separation from a loved one. All of the techniques I will suggest, therefore, will be capable of being applied to any of the other isolated situations—no matter how isolated they get.

The sailor, when at sea, is in a position somewhat like that of an incarcerated individual. A sailor might be quick to say the land-prisoner actually has it far better in one respect: conjugal visits. So if a sailor wants to look at his or her situation in the most depressing way possible, the sailor can say, 'I'm in jail in a floating prison, not only without the

Part 5: Thriving in the Single Life (in Splendid Solitude)

comfort of conjugal visits, but without even a single Plexiglas-separated meeting with somebody I miss.' Well, as I say, a 'floating prison' is really not an outrageous way to characterize the situation. The reality, however, is that it is not a prison: there is no stigma attached to having been this kind of inmate, you are making a living doing work you presumably enjoy doing. As for the prison aspect, such isolation has all the useful features of land jails and none of the unavoidable negatives. Yes you read that right—even real prisons have the potential (which is rarely made use of by the prisoners) to do a prisoner good by way of self-improvement in many areas, including present and future happiness.

In fact even the real prisoner's stigma can be rendered irrelevant if he or she realizes their opportunity early, sees the pointlessness of self-pity, and works out and sticks to a system for improvement. Ironically, the useful features of prisons include several things people generally cannot arrange to have (even if they wanted to) when free: isolation from social distractions, mental and physical freedom from the pursuit of money and food, no car bus or other mechanized travel. These enforced freedoms can be just what the doctor ordered for the prisoners who take advantage of them, giving them a break from the vicious circles they have established in the outside world. If nothing else they will have a chance to reflect on their life; and, if they can avoid falling into traps of self-pity and bitterness, it is likely they will come to see the big picture of their life much more clearly than ever before.

Nonetheless the same is true in the less extreme case of the sailor at sea, and even more true in the far less extreme case of the person who is between relationships in a commonplace way. Even though this latter person has to think about money etc, he or she has no severe limitations imposed on the expression of their singleness. They can develop themselves in their freedom using a world's worth of resources. And there is certainly a lot less to pity yourself over, whatever the cause of being between relationships: your life is not put on hold in any way. And so the ordinary person between relationships is in a position requiring for success little more than the proper outlook, a plan, and a moderate amount of self-discipline.

To return to the sailor's situation, he or she will require a greater measure

Happy Between Relationships

of self-discipline, especially in forming and maintaining the proper outlook. It is undoubtedly hard to convince yourself when in the middle of the ocean that you are doing anything but biding your time until you return to civilization. But if the potential benefits of this time of isolation from the usual family and social circles are kept constantly before the mind, and if they are seen as real benefits and not just glorified time-killers—then we're in business. These benefits include:

> 1) uncluttered mental space in which to give extended thought to fundamental issues;
>
> 2) uncluttered mental space in which to plan and begin challenging projects.

Let's take a look at what each of these benefits might give rise to.

- Giving extended thought to fundamental issues

This might lead to:

> - a new improved attitude toward a loved one;
> - a new improved attitude toward yourself;
> - a better understanding of what you are ready for in life and how to get it;
> - a better understanding of how people, civilization, and nature work, and how all three interact and *should* interact.

These improvements, of course, can be immensely aided by the reading of good books (like this one!). And these ideas can only lead to the flourishing of the next item:

- Planning and beginning challenging projects

This might lead to:

> - mastery of a particular subject, possibly leading to...
> - expert status in that subject, through...

Part 5: Thriving in the Single Life (in Splendid Solitude)

- the invention of something, either a process, machine, design, article, book, which might lead to...
- a promotion or new career.

And if it leads to none of the above, at least it will have added an interesting and absorbing pursuit bound to increase daily enjoyment, intensity and learning.

The whole key in the case of enforced isolation, as in the case of any length of time between relationships, is to consider that time *just* as valuable as time spent with loved ones. A quotation attributed to Charles Darwin goes "A man who dares to waste one hour of time has not discovered the value of life." Of course if you don't have a purpose, a goal in sight, there is little possibility of not wasting most of your available time.

My personal solution is to have a goal—but also goals. This means that in most everything I do when between relationships (or in them for that matter) I try to make it fun, interesting, challenging instead of just going through the motions. This means there is a constant reminder before you that you have the power to seize happiness at any time, instead of having to wait until the time, place, and person are just right. So that sometimes even when performing the most common routines of life I set goals. Closing the window, for instance, then becomes a kind of wacky spice as I try to think of some subtle variation on my last closing. However, spice is unpalatable eaten by itself, and in order for it to please there must be a substantial and meaty main course for it to blend into.

Although the closest I've ever been to being a sailor is going deep sea fishing and taking the ferry, I think it might not be too presumptuous for me to make a few general assumptions. One of these general assumptions about the sailor's facts of life when at sea would be that he or she is restricted to a very limited physical space. In other words they can't go for a walk or a drive or a bike ride worth mentioning. Nor can they go to a friend's house or take a getaway weekend. They can't even pick up and sleep downstairs on a whim. And this restriction is related to another defining restriction—an inescapable unvarying daily

Happy Between Relationships

routine. I'll presume to no further knowledge of the seafaring life than these two pretty obvious assumptions.

Now what good can come from a situation seemingly designed to make you go crazy—even before you factor in your separation from loved ones? Let's take a look at some of the buried possibilities.

First of all, since there are these built-in limitations, at least the sailor has a ready-made framework around which to weave his or her creative ideas. And what kind of creative ideas could possibly amount to anything in the circumstances? Well, with there being a lot of routine, done in routine places and at routine times, it seems to me that there are three ways of viewing the little free time available. Two of them are likely to be productive of benefits, the other productive of nothing much. This last is the middle or easiest road; it consists in soothing your consciousness with the usual television, radio, games, movies, alcohol, chitchat, etc. The other two ways have nothing to do with soothing—they are about *stimulating* your brain. After all, what is being soothed—just being bored; and boredom is the best breeding place for negative dismal thoughts: nothing much, in other words.

The other two techniques of using free time are based on attitudes containing a degree of extremism. I agree with Lafcadio Hern, the nineteenth century American writer, who said, "I believe very strongly in extremes; and I am quite sure that all progress in the world, whether literary, or scientific, or religious, or political, or social, has been obtained only with the assistance of extremes." I might add to the list personal happiness. The situation in which the sailor at sea finds himself or herself is one of extremes by necessity; all the easier then perhaps for the sailor to reap the benefits of the positive varieties of extreme behavior. The extremism of the day's routine might be extended into free hours with regular goal-driven sessions of, say, study of a particular subject in order to master it or body building. The other technique would be the opposite form of extremism, that is to explore many different areas of interest which you never had time or discipline enough to explore on land, say, the history of the U.S Navy, literature, how the stock market works, astronomy. The goal of the latter activities might be simply to broaden your outlook or knowledge.

Part 5: Thriving in the Single Life (in Splendid Solitude)

Of course for both the person in the extreme situation and the person who is not there is no good in putting yourself under continual strain. A time of relaxation is essential to mental and physical good health. But does this require total mental and physical *rest?* For someone new to a given extreme situation this may well be the case: a sailor, to use our extreme example, might well be seasick much of the first day at sea and be totally incapacitated for everything but rest that evening. However, for people fairly well established in the routine of their given circumstances, *whether these are extreme or otherwise,* I believe that relaxation, and even rest, can and should contain a *measure* of vigorous activity. Again, why should you have to be bored in order to recover from the effects of the day's work?

The sailor, at the finish of an especially hard day's work, looks forward, no doubt, to the end of his or her duties and a refuge from outside demands. Outside demands—this is the key phrase. This accounts for much of the fatigue of the sailor. This accounts for much of the fatigue of most anybody at the end of the day's work. The difference is that the sailor has no possibility of submerging himself or herself in the comforting atmosphere of a loving family or relationship on returning from work. And yet the major comfort still exists, if it is recognized, of being free from outside, professional demands. (Of course the sailor is also free of the mild demands of relationships as well.) It is my contention that, even being exhausted and in circumstances cut off from the comforts of loved ones, a person needs little more than to find themselves at their own disposal to be substantially reenergized. This person just needs something exciting to apply themselves to.

So, largely depending on the way you look at it, you can be miserable when isolated from key relationships; or you can be, possibly, just as happy—at least more in control of the elements that compose your happiness. That is the built-in weakness of any relationship with a person other than yourself: you only control half of it. And no matter what your degree of influence over the other, no matter how well-matched and harmonious you are compared to other relationships, the other regularly behaves in less than precise accordance with your wishes. To complicate the situation even more, no possible behavior on the other's part could ever be entirely pleasing—even in intent. For even were a

Happy Between Relationships

person to show complete obedience to your wishes, you would soon begin to wish they were not such a jellyfish and be irritated they never asserted their own personalities.

The person who is compelled to be separated from their relationship, or removed from the locations where the possibility of finding one is a reality, is in a position to discover—or miss completely—a new world. Here a Columbus can find a partner he or she can—not without continual effort though—be nearly 100 percent pleased with: yourself. But, as with all opportunities for great rewards, there is an equal opportunity for great punishment—self-punishment in this case. This is so because there is no one to correct non-productive thinking or behavior but yourself.

Even though it is hard, as everyone knows and has confirmed every day of their lives, to control yourself, it is much easier when you are by yourself. And while you are likely to sink toward despair if you have made the person left behind the cornerstone of your happiness, yet just making a sustained effort not to is likely to be enough to prevent it. I believe the solution is basically a simple one because what you are dealing with is basic and simple compared with what you had been dealing with: another human being with his or her countless, unpredictable thoughts words actions—on top of your own. And although it may seem selfish to concern yourself entirely with yourself and what is needed to please you, it absolutely is not. Doing what is necessary to be as happy as possible is the best thing you could do for people special to you and anybody you come in contact with for that matter. Because happiness equals health, both mental and physical. It also equals every kind of good treatment of others special or not: fairness, patience, forgiveness, generosity, willingness to listen, etc.

Now let's examine the benefits of the best friend of anybody who is alone—for any reason, any amount of time.

Part 5: Thriving in the Single Life (in Splendid Solitude)

I love to lose myself in other men's minds.

—Charles Lamb, writer

Love books; they will teach you to respect yourselves and others, and fill the mind and the heart with love for the world and man.

Even if hostile to your beliefs, any book that has been written in honesty, out of love of people, out of good will, is admirable.

—Maksim Gorki, novelist

60.

Reading Books

Reading books is not just another activity that may contribute to happiness in the single life, it is an essential one. Perhaps *the* essential one. A book is never just a form of entertainment or a load of information, it is essentially a living thing, the best part of one or a few human beings in concentrate. The equivalent of a two hour high-speed conversation. Magazines and newspapers are full of informed no-nonsense chat—high speed connections, as quickly terminated, with the edited essence of human beings.

What is the great benefit of examining various people's minds in this way? There are several. Here are two key ones:

1) On finishing a thoroughly read and understood book, you have become something of an expert—in fact a double expert. You will have achieved a measure of expertise not only on the subject of the book, but just as much on the author himself or herself.

2) The more you know well the more the joy you have in contemplation, being more confident in your speculations; because knowledge in depth on one subject or person always contains clues to the nature of all subjects and persons.

Additional benefits of examining minds through books

Reading gives you a sense of various cultures different from your own. You need not read a book on travels in faraway lands to experience this either. Even if you read a book on the New York Stock Exchange of

Part 5: Thriving in the Single Life (in Splendid Solitude)

last year, it is quite possible, from your home in say Texas or Illinois, to become entranced by the substantial differences in attitude speech and life-style that inevitably exist between people so separated by distance that they rarely mix. And these differences are even more fascinatingly pronounced when time is the separation rather than geography.

When you read a book that was written a decade or more ago, again no matter what the subject matter, you are instantly transported to a culture wholly different from the one outside your door. Not only different but dead, and never to be revived in precisely the same form again. Moreover one that can be visited no other way than by that book. Even a film or television dramatization of that very book would be bogus because made by people living in a different time; the author of the book is living and breathing what he or she is writing about. In the case of a historical novel or movie adaptation of a book, you much more strongly feel the life of the culture in which it was written than that of its dramatic setting. And it is indeed through the author, his or her choice of words, the aspects of the subject which are focused on, the overall attitude, that this cultural world is transmitted—not merely through the things and events described. (An example of this would be the hopeful and idealistic writing immediately after World War Two, and the anti-establishment tone as the cold war escalated.)

Books are portable. Though portable televisions exist, and even if they come to be commonly made to be worn wristwatch style, they will never be as convenient or at least as enjoyable as a book is while on the go. First of all a book is by its nature more enjoyable than television, given that the book and the program are both of good quality (which I shall discuss further in a moment). As for convenience, a book is something you can carry with you anywhere you go—including the shower if you are wacky enough and have a zip-lock plastic bag and a book that will fit inside while open. During a wait of any length, you can reach for your book and fill the time very easily without bothering anybody; or if you wish to avoid a conversation with somebody pretended involvement in your book might possibly save you (not from certain brash souls however).

Reading books *must* be an active pleasure, while watching television

Happy Between Relationships

can be a passive one. When you read a book, even if it is just for entertainment, you get an intellectual workout, imagining characters and situations, grasping ideas, analyzing the meanings of various sentence structures and assimilating new words and expressions. When you watch television you may well be intellectually stimulated, however no discipline is required so that the vast majority of the details need not be absorbed to keep watching. Television entertainment, moreover, requires no imagination (the pictures are provided) no discernment (laugh tracks tell you what is funny, ominous music tells you when something sinister is about to happen).

It might be argued that television is relaxing. Well I agree with that and sometimes relax with the help of TV myself. It is also educational, as I have mentioned before. The key is to not let it dominate your leisure hours; and perhaps the best way to do this is to become devoted to books. A good way to break the spell of television is to keep your favorite books within reach while watching TV. Reading them during muted commercials will remind you that your books are more interesting and soon take you to the delicious silence of your reading room.

Reading promotes writing down your thoughts. This is so because you tend to think more verbally after consuming a lot of words, especially if they are contained in carefully structured sentences. And with an expanded vocabulary from constant reading, almost inevitably ways of expressing certain thoughts will suggest themselves, too valuable to be left unexpressed or to be merely paraphrased in conversation. And once the habit is established of writing down inspired thoughts, it is only a small step to the habit of writing in general. Everyone can write, and it is an activity with big possible rewards for everyone who does it, not just the professional or would-be professional.

Using writing to induce 'flow'

For instance, writing is one of the most effective activities for inducing 'flow.' This is a concept formulated by psychologist Mihaly Csikszentmihalyi (pronounced chick-SENT-me-hi) after observing artists and other creative persons at work. It describes that state which everyone has experienced where time passes very quickly—where in

Part 5: Thriving in the Single Life (in Splendid Solitude)

fact you actually lose awareness of the passage of time. When you write you effectively check out of your conscious mind. Leaving its nagging preoccupations and even its outward sights and sensory computations in the distant background, you check in to your subconscious—a hotel whose windows are not windows but mirrors which reflect vast inward landscapes. Given the great gift of being set free to explore the Haunted Mansion of your brain, you quickly find the opportunity enthralling as you find that within this Haunted Mansion is contained the rest of Disneyland. You lose yourself and ticking time as you explore a virtually unlimited number of high-speed theme rides and mental adventures of every possible description. And when it's time to come home from this amusement park, you needn't face the freeway: all it takes is for the phone to ring, the cat to put in a request for dinner, or simply for the 'flow' to temporarily run dry—and there you are, back in your living room wondering pleasantly what you should have for dinner.

You sit down to dinner with:

- the liberated feeling that you have used your brain at its highest level;
- that you have demonstrated talent;
- that you have remembered things long forgotten and discovered things you didn't know you knew;
- that you have saved part of the best part of yourself, which if properly preserved could outlive you indefinitely.

And from here you might go with another potential 'flow.'

61.

The Computer and Happiness

Today people socialize in a much more selective way than they did even ten years ago. The explosion of the AIDS epidemic coinciding with the explosion of personal computers and their astronomical social and professional possibilities, did much to bring this about. They go to chat rooms instead of bar rooms, checkout a person's picture on their Web site instead of their bodies on the dance floor, and dispatch electronic messages to friends relating the essence of what they have to say instead of spending a whole evening in their actual presence conveying it in spoken dribs and drabs. Not to suggest that people have stopped altogether making contact the old fashioned way; but it is clear that vast and growing numbers of people do less of it than people used to do. Sometimes they even rent a movie instead of finding someone to go to the theater with.

Now take someone who is involved professionally socially playfully (through video game software) with their computer. What are the positive and negative implications of this activity on that person's actual physical relationships? I mean how does this impact on the person he or she is dating or married to? If without one how does the computer help or hinder her or him in their desires of finding one? More specific to the purpose of this book, what is the effect of a computer on the way someone recovers from a breakup and on his or her happiness during the time between relationships? These are questions whose answers have a great bearing on determining the healthiest role for the computer to play in the lives of people. And as to the question of whether computers will necessarily play a part in most people's happiness or unhappiness there is no question.

Part 5: Thriving in the Single Life (in Splendid Solitude)

Remember when the Heaven's Gate cult mass suicide was in the news? Cult experts would appear on television and pronounce the 39 cultists "socially inept, socially starved," desperate and lost childlike suckers. However, what set them apart from previous childlike suckers was that they were "technologically proficient" childlike suckers: they designed web sites for a living. On top of designing web sites for others they had their own, into which massive labor must have gone, as it was lavished with every digital allurement including hundreds of pages of documentation of cult information.

Now "socially inept, socially starved" are the kind of terms in which computer users—especially before computers went mainstream—are sometimes described. The phrases "computer geek" and "computer nerd" have long since entered the language, used abbreviated to "geek" or "nerd" mostly by the users themselves of each other—these days. It is more of a joke than anything else these days, because high tech expertise is rapidly going from a sign of a weird robot-like mentality to a mark of membership in the cultural elite. And yet it is understood by all that there is at least a grain of truth in this characterization of the computer expert—that on average they are not among the most gifted of party animals. There is nothing wrong, of course, with not being a party animal, either by choice or by ineptitude. Neither is there anything wrong with being somewhat on the introverted side. The important question to be answered here is when does the internet stop being a social boon for introverts and start doing them social harm and stunting their happiness?

Let's take a close look at how both introverts and extroverts can benefit from the internet.

62.

The Internet and the Person Between Relationships

The World Wide Web is another planet. But not in the way Jupiter is another planet: a place we can't relate to even in the remotest way. The WWW is another planet the way the Twilight Zone was another planet: familiar in many respects, but humming with an overall eeriness, booby-trapped with hypnotic curiosities. The another planet metaphor can be continued for probably another ten pages, but I'll cut it off here by concluding that, like the Twilight Zone, it's a nice place to watch but I wouldn't want to live there. However, this is clearly the 'virtual' residence for many people who are between relationships.

It becomes for some not only the place where they spend most of their waking hours, it becomes the place where they live, in the sense of feel alive. As it is a vital work tool or their business itself for exploding numbers of people today, many people are referring to it continually at work; then they go to it for entertainment when the workday is done and undoubtedly during lunch breaks sometimes too. Now, though this is obviously excessive, the answer is not plain to the question: "Is this bad?" This is simply because there is an enormous amount and variety of entertainment value on the web; even a wealth of opportunities for socializing and (in theory at least) meeting people. In short, the Web is a monster, a glorious entertaining monster of the proportions of TV and beyond, with tentacles draped all around the curious user, almost inescapable for the lonely.

But this book denies the validity of the idea of loneliness and is about techniques to transform it into a productive emotion. So let's face the question head on as to when and if the Web surfer might be depriving

Part 5: Thriving in the Single Life (in Splendid Solitude)

himself or herself of real happiness by not tearing out of those terrible tentacles. However, first of all it might be asked whether it isn't all just a waste of a person's precious free time? Well, as a fairly frequent surfer myself, I think it can safely be considered far from a waste of time under any circumstances. Even if you think entertainment by itself is throwing away valuable time (as I do not incidentally), there is no need to worry about a dearth of educational entertainment on the Web; and unlike TV the best programs are always available for you to immerse yourself in. But this is not intended to be a commercial for the Web, and I have no doubt that it's power to hypnotize is an insidious danger.

This being the case, when and how should the person in the vulnerable position between relationships finally disconnect? When, as it seems to me, is the more difficult question, in terms of the number of hours use per day to be considered too many. Answering the 'how' question will undoubtedly give a feel, if not an exact number of hours, for the length of a healthy visit. The best way to break the hold of anything that has you in its addictive embrace is to find something else that is even more exciting. But this is not as difficult as it sounds. For an alcoholic this is something as simple as being sober. Once the alcoholic has conquered the craving, both the idea and the feeling of being clear-minded are as thrilling as it ever was to be drunk. For the person who is using the Web for the purposes of a cocoon between relationships, escape is easier if not simpler: there is no chemical dependency to overcome. The same goes for the other major glutton of an individual's free time: television. All that is needed is something new and exciting, which needn't be something spectacular, because the novelty alone may surpass the thrill of the Web routine in prospect.

The novelty of any simple change in the evening's routine, such as going out to do almost anything instead of staying in to surf the Web or watch TV, can lead to a rediscovery of old interests and discovery of new adventures. Just going for a walk to a friend's house, or simply around the block, if you never do these things, can begin to break the spell cast by monitors and start developing a taste for creative instead of routine disposing of the evening's time. Once a person begins creatively structuring their free time, the events which result cannot help being varied and continually interesting and even productive,

Happy Between Relationships

because a series of goals automatically spring to life, calling for intense and structured pursuit. The Web, therefore, will come to be used for shorter but more purposeful and exciting sessions, and not by any means be reduced to nothing but a work tool.

Part 5: Thriving in the Single Life (in Splendid Solitude)

...The computer, a companion without emotional demands, offers a compromise. You can be a loner, but never alone. You can interact, but need never feel velnerable to another person.

—Sherry Turkle, academic

Television's strongest point is that it brings personalities into our hearts, not abstractions into our heads.

—Neil Postman, writer

63.

Good Uses of the Web and TV for Those Between Relationships

When used with moderation, on a take-it-or-leave-it basis, I have found both the Web and TV to be excellent forms of entertainment as well as terrific ways to learn and grow as a person. Considered solely as ways to increase general or specific knowledge, they are in some respects even superior to reading books. People remember information conveyed by pictures much better than if they only read about it, for one thing. Of course this is only true if the viewer of the pictures or motion pictures musters some concentration. Also the knowledge thus gained, especially in the case of TV, may have none too whopping a practical value. But so what! Life isn't only about learning useful information. Watching a sitcom a soap or a sporting event can be tremendously entertaining, with lots of healthy laughing, dramatic tension, and cheering. What's more, entertainment can be made use of too for creative projects (as I discussed in the Chapter "Making happy progress in solitude" earlier this Part. I mentioned the power of seeing a good movie in "Using media contact as relationship substitutes" to start off this Part.)

If you have had your fill of TV and have a computer and modem, you might take a whirl in this alternative entertainment and learning medium. The Internet and especially the Web provide a nice alternative to TV on the one side and reading a book on the other. It fits snugly in between these giant entertainment and learning media as a glorious blend of the two. If your head is spinning from watching to many hyper-cutting TV commercials or frantic action movie sequences, you can turn to the Web for cool calming still photographs, or colorful but composed and beautifully silent marginal animation. The human population, too, is sparse regarding pictures of actual bodies, which is sometimes a relief

Part 5: Thriving in the Single Life (in Splendid Solitude)

after the bustling crowds of TV. With the star of most every program being not a charismatic human face but a typeface. And this of course is where the book aspect comes in. And remember, there are several differences in Web reading which may refresh you.

First, because it's the most basic, is the simple fact that when you read from a computer monitor you can sit in a natural, relaxed position. Book reading, though it can be a snuggly experience when you curl up with a good one, though it is more versatile in terms of choice of places and positions in which to read, has some minor quirks which the Web can liberate you from. When you read a book you always end up looking down, often quite severely floorward, because if you hold it at normal eye level your arm gets tired. Your neck, in an effort to ease the burden of the eye muscles, bows your head. Then there's the aforementioned arm fidgeting the book around, and the hand worrying about holding the pages back and keeping the book adjusted to the optimum reading angle. Silly little inconveniences I'll admit (and you don't notice them if you don't have a computer), but it can be very refreshing to unbend your neck and let your hands dangle on your lap as you consume your next paragraph.

And then there is the essence of the Web, which also happens to be the greatest gift high technology ever gave to those who like to read, as well as anybody with some of the explorer in them: the hyperlink. These underlined words or phrases have largely accounted for the transformation of the geekdom of computerland into a place so hip that 'surfing' is used to describe recreational Web use. While surfing may be a pretty good stretch as a description of what happens when one goes a-hyperlinking, it is still a good indication of the size of the dose of fun and freedom injected into user veins by the advent of the 'link'. By just clicking on an underlined word, you're off—whirling through cyberspace for an instant before being plunked down in another private screening room, the screen blank but soon unveiling it's contents one by one like a cyber-stripper. From here you can blast off yet again on another turbo surfboard to whatever destination the Webmaster considers usefully related or just a nice mini-vacation.

All of this hyperlink action is full of intrigue and suspense and all the

Happy Between Relationships

things that go to make up a first class adventure. Combine this with the speed of the changes of scenery and a variety as wide as the general population, and you get a pretty interesting toy. There is certainly something there for everyone—-from discussions and journals of the latest theories in any scientific discipline you can name (and many you can't); to personal Web pages of the silliest caliber, queasily reminiscent of home movies; to virtual art galleries of painting, photography, computer graphics; to voluminous works of reference, providing every kind of practical and general information; to on-line dating services, chat rooms with topics from A to Z, personal adds, pornography; to the almost up-to-the-minute news in every field.

So with all this to choose from don't be conservative, be creative! Boldly go where you've never gone before—then boldly disconnect!

Easing a TV addict into a habit of reading

While both Web addiction and TV addiction are bad when consuming, having all your free time consumed by TV is worse and much easier to have happen to you. The key difference between these two square boxes that you stare into is that with one you must eventually apply concentration to stay interested. Graphics and hyperlinks provide a tasty sauce but little meat; the meat of the medium is old-fashioned written words, stuffed with new-fangled technology. The meat the TV addict finds so congenial does not contain the rich protein of the written word. The TV addict makes do with a kind of soy protein equivalent. With no written words, concentration tends to take a vacation, replaced by, at the worst, a warm fuzzy sense of awareness much like a dial tone.

For someone who is used to turning on the TV when they get home from work and turning it off when they're ready to go to bed, the transition to sitting silently with a book during the same time is kind of like going from a hot tub to dive into a cold swimming pool. The Web is an excellent way to fall under the spell of the written sentence. As a graphics-intensive Web page splashes across your monitor, you can almost hear the echoes from glitzy TV variety shows. And what you actually do hear is also TV-like. The frantic sound of the page being loaded is reassuringly like that of the intros of news programs.

Part 5: Thriving in the Single Life (in Splendid Solitude)

However, when you are tired of frantic sounds of all kinds, there is an excellent way to escape.

64.

Outdoor Paths to Happiness Between Relationships

Sometimes getting away from frustration or boredom or conflict is as simple as stepping outside into the fresh air. Nearly everybody uses and appreciates the fresh air outside their doors. Maybe it is not made use of as much as it should be for calming or other purposes, yet it is resorted to, probably unconsciously by many, universally. And yet the air is not the only thing that is fresh outside their door. Trees, grass, birds, bugs, the sky (certain parts of it at least, even in Los Angeles), the sun, all of these natural things are guaranteed to be fresh year round, even providing a variety of fresh forms with the changing seasons. (The same cannot always be said of the people passing through the fresh air, however; doubly so when they are in cars, making the fresh air less fresh with a combination of exhaust fumes and grim faces.) So why has the common expression been limited to just the air? I mean why wasn't it, "I'm going to step outside to get some fresh air, sky, trees, bugs and birds."? It's my belief that the whole package may as well be turned to your advantage and profit in terms of well-being and happiness.

And since the trees, birds and so forth outside your door are only part of the wide selection available, why not combine your interest in them with another terrific activity to perform solo—-traveling? The great outdoors is still pretty great circa 1997, with state, regional, and national parks and forests still holding their own in the U.S. and still available for recreational use by the general public. However, someone might say that going to a place by yourself where there are no people sounds like a pretty good way to make yourself feel really lonely. That same person might then go on to add what they think clinches the

Part 5: Thriving in the Single Life (in Splendid Solitude)

inadvisability of such plans for the person between relationships. With the sympathetic pain of their expression, they would silently remind you that any beauty such a place may contain will only bring home to you the embarrassing fact that you are not romantically involved with anyone.

To me this is utterly backwards thinking, and on top of that it shows a total absence of understanding of who human beings are and what basic elements make up their pleasures. Though I am not an anthropologist, I have done some reading and thinking on the subject over the years, and I think I may advance one or two mainly common sense theories.

Mankind evolved to where we are today from very primitive, cave-dwelling tribes. These great, great, great (add ten or twelve more 'greats' and you'll start to get warm) ancestors of ours lived in this condition for many thousands of years. In fact they lived in this nature boy style for so long that their senses became highly attuned to receiving messages from all-natural occurrences. For example, their sense of hearing could tell them at once whether a given sound signaled a danger, a sought-after object, or a non-threat to their safety. Dangers aplenty lurked as well as thundered about in the open in those days, a kind of 'original stress' that makes the kind we suffer from in the modern world look like a vacation at Disneyworld. Nevertheless there were compensations, and none too shaby ones. There were no fences, no "No trespassing" signs, no restriction to a few small public parks and public shops and restaurants in a sprawling city and suburban area. They could explore anything they were capable of walking swimming swinging climbing or running for their lives to, never in danger of encountering a locked door or a security guard telling them this is a restricted access area. They had freedom in its most pristine sense.

In fact their cup (which usually meant their hands) was running over with pristines. And general pristine-ness entails for the semi-naked low-technology-using human being the stressful preoccupation with defense strategies mentioned above. In other words our primitive ancestors knew where they stood, and the dangerous and the harmless and the beneficial were ever before their mental eye, danger probably seeming most real— the opposite of the way we perceive reality. Their lives were usually

Happy Between Relationships

short, they were engulfed in their environment, not masters of it, they were just a part of the huge organism of the Earth. They could hardly have had a single one of the pretensions to special status that we take for granted today. All of this contributed, I'd be more than willing to bet, to a thorough appreciation of peaceful, relatively relaxed moments. But also of the places and activities in which they normally found them; as well as the individual organisms and elements that seemed to express or symbolize these relaxed feelings.

This meant that when they found themselves sitting beside a protective fire at sunset on a balmy summer evening, it was natural to be soothed on a later date by the mere appearance of a sunset. The circumstances might have been less secure and comfortable, might have been downright hairy, and yet the sunset retained some if not all of its ability to soothe the spirits. Especially if the scene of safety and comfort had been repeated a number of times, as these evening fires undoubtedly were. The other typical features of those rare blissful evenings, when the weather and beasts teamed up to give them a break, also undoubtedly acquired a certain charm. The lazy whispering of the trees and other foliage as the now stirring now dying breezes came and went; the sight of smaller creatures being much more nervous, watchful, and active than they seemed to need to be just now; insects darting in every direction in excited confusion around the fire; the stars beginning to pop into the sky as bright, clear, winking mysteries.

As I have mentioned, this life-style of mostly unrelenting natural stress and some natural ecstasy lasted for great heaping piles of generations of humankind—ten thousand years worth or more. Their accommodations stayed pretty much the same, and the cast of characters in all the dramas (most of them nonfictional) were somewhat limited by today's standards. The lead role was always filled by all-mighty all-beautiful Nature; the supporting cast filled by Humankind with their big brains and ever-so-slowly growing collection of knowledge and low-tech tools and weapons. After something on the order of ten billion performances of minor variations on this theme, you can imagine that Humankind came to know their role pretty well. And of course, with the nifty supercomputers they lugged around in their heads, they eventually started to make headway against Nature. And yet, sharp as

Part 5: Thriving in the Single Life (in Splendid Solitude)

they were, they also developed a strong appreciation for Nature, which became somewhat ingrained after all that experience of her.

Now let's jump forward to the Humankind of today. We live mostly in cities these days in the U.S.; whether they are big or small, amid inner congestion or outer suburbia, on Main Street or Manhattan, most places where people live today are cities—not farms or small towns or isolated settlements. This means that the majority of people do not have daily contact with raw Nature. And even if they did it still would not compare with the total, day-and-night submersion of the cave dweller in Nature's sounds, smells, and scenes. Does this indicate that people have outgrown Nature, that aside from the necessities of life she supplies (food, water, materials for building cities) people can afford to take Nature or leave her? I don't think so.

Our cities are in many respects our dreams of paradise come true, no doubt about it. They have fabulous conveniences, a growing number of entertainment options, countless opportunities for social interaction both meaningful and casual, even a few scattered human renditions of Nature herself. And yet, every dream can quickly slip into nightmare mode without warning; and every dream, however sweet, has nightmarish moments, flashes of insanity, the inexplicable and the weird. These moments or periods in a modern city dweller's life are I believe often no more than the effects of living in a city—a 99% human-created environment. Why should this be a problem? Remember those dozens of generations of Nature boys and girls I mentioned? They were camping so long they achieved a cliche! They became *one with Nature* in a sense.

In fact in all of their senses. Evolution took hold of all five of their senses and designed and refined them as we continued to distance ourselves from the apes mentally and physically—always to work in better and better harmony with what we were up against: raw Nature. Such sounds as Airplane engines make, such smells as gasoline, sights like music videos, experiences like being in the middle of a stadium packed with fifty thousand concert goers—these things were very *very* rarely encountered by those of our ancestors who lived in caves. The result is that our constant exposure to loud noises, and even certain

Happy Between Relationships

noises that we consider to be on a reasonable decibel level, can contribute heavily to putting us on edge. This constant bombardment of noise is not found on a daily basis in Nature; and where Nature is noisy (wind, heavy rain) there is less annoyance because of the ancient positive association of these events with the storms which yearly renewed life.

Nature in its undeveloped state has silence in the starring role, with noises as supporting actors; supporting actors, moreover, with very limited roles. And so it goes regarding all else which is fed to the senses in her domain: Nature commands it silently and subtly. The sense-scene appears to be never-changing—with pictures, scents, sounds seemingly fixed and simple. Change sneaks up on the observer with a subtle lead-in—-like a cloud bank on an originally cloudless day, heralded by a slightly accelerated breeze; or it can be found on a closer inspection of the seemingly fixed landscape (like the discovery that a log you are about to sit on is covered with ants). Action, in other words, is always present, there is always a feast for the senses, only most of the time it is buffet style.

In modern cities, however, the eating style is all to often force-feeding. Car horns, people complaining, red green and yellow lights; and the sign-circuit from "stay off the grass" to " sorry, we're closed". Many of the city messages need to be as clear as possible and so their uniform appearance is universal. This, though it is admirable from an efficiency standpoint, does not lend itself to interesting or attractive variations—except in the case of person to person messages. A stop sign is a stop sign—it means stop and has the potential to mean very little else. The lack of subtlety is a characteristic unique to cities, and one of the features of city life—along with the general noise level—which I think everybody could appreciate to take a break from.

This being the case, why do some people feel they would be lonely if they went hiking or sailing by themselves? I think it boils down to the habit of staying continually connected to other people in the city. And at the heart of human nature are the tendencies to be social and habit-forming. The explanation for this lies once again with our early relatives: they needed to stick close together in well organized groups to survive.

Part 5: Thriving in the Single Life (in Splendid Solitude)

The formation of strong habits insured that each member of the social organization fulfilled their role in supporting the group; teamwork which was necessary for vulnerable man to compete against stronger faster animals. And so people sit around, when left to themselves on a weekend, feeling vaguely annoyed on a beautiful day watching a rerun. Instead they could get in the car and go to a nearby state park, where they could feel physical and (with the right attitude going in) mental freedom.

Another way to physical and mental freedom follows.

65.

Exercising Your Happiness

Exercise has become fashionable among non-athletes in the last twenty years or so. Even so, according to recent surveys, only approximately 1/4 of the U.S. population can be classified as regular exercisers in 1997. Nonetheless most of the remaining sedentary and semi-sedentary people are willing to admit that they have been convinced, by all the scientific studies and onslaught of media images of attractive exercisers, that exercise can be beneficial. Probably, since they are not regularly involved in exercise, their information condenses to something like: it will cause you to lose unsightly pounds if you do enough; also there is a health benefit. These arguments for exercising are true enough; yet I can see how they might soon lose force to motivate. The first seems to require the dedication of a marine, while the second offers you a vague improvement in health when you are not sick and actually feel pretty good.

There are far more attractive and compelling arguments for vigorous regular exercise. I will get to them in a moment. They are all highly practical reasons, offering us glittering prizes with heaping amounts of substance beneath the glitter. First, however, I want to give very briefly an exercise for exercise's sake philosophy.

Exercise is not only maintenance of the body: it is respect for your body and yourself. And those with real reverence for life, especially their own, have much of the foundation for happiness in place. Exercise is a way to enhance appreciation of your body and life. At the same time it's my belief humankind should take a peek from time to time at the behavior of their fellow mammals. We are alone in this wide circle of warm-blooded beings in not respecting our own bodies. With other

Part 5: Thriving in the Single Life (in Splendid Solitude)

mammals the body comes first: the day revolves around strategies for supplying it with optimal nutrition, and sufficient periods for rest and cleaning. People, on the other hand, in their usual complexly perverse way, manage their lives seemingly with a view toward abusing their bodies from as many angles as possible. We stay up too late, drink to excess concoctions containing mild poisons, inhibit the performance of our lungs with smoke, eat vast amounts of nutrients that we know will not be used, and, the final insult, withhold from the body it's one fighting chance against these enemies—exercise. Nobody's perfect, and I myself have certainly been guilty of some of these abuses off and on. But whatever trauma the mind may be going through, at least respect the body enough to give it a potent means of self defense in exercise.

Now the statement that exercise is the body's due in life is not going to get anyone past their problems with doing exercise on a regular basis. But finding ways of enjoying it will. Yes it may surprise some people, but a good workout can be one of the things you look forward to doing in your day. Actually *look forward* to. And not only because by doing it you will have cause to feel "good" in a self-satisfied way, like a student handing in extra credit work. Mainly because after a workout you *will* feel " good" in the sense that your body will be radiating positive vibes like the sun. Good feelings so powerful even that gloomy part of the brain, the cerebral cortex, the irritable thinking center, can't resist and begins chirping cheerful thoughts. However this ecstasy is only possible if the other parts of the process are enjoyed enough for themselves to be done well, which means *intensely*. And to develop an intensity for exercise it is most helpful to realize why exercising gives ten times the return of any other possible investment of an hour:

- Establishes a tone for the day. If you like the idea, as I do, that "each day the world is born anew for him who takes it rightly" as occurred to James Russell Lowell, then why not set a vibrant fresh 'like new' tone for yourself every new morning. And I'm not doing a soap commercial; I'm doing an exercise commercial. There is no more reliable way to set it, no more vivid terms in which to set it, than those of exercise. A good workout has the seeming effect on your bloodstream of breaking a series of beaver dams, clearing the way for a born-free gush.

Happy Between Relationships

This freed blood is liquid vibrancy.

- Lets you feel strength and surging life. Even those of us who are ashamed of our body's abilities, and so reduce them even further by neglecting their maintenance, can feel the power. (If you think you are too skinny or too fat to possibly be seen exercising, tell yourself you are being silly. Silly to the point of needlessly and severely limiting your possibilities of being happy. 90 percent of the time shame is sheer folly and does nothing but paralyze your ability to do perfectly reasonable actions. When it keeps you from freely and openly taking care of yourself, for example. No one cares that your bodyweight is under or over your ideal, no matter how much it may be.) You are alive and you are healthy, you have muscle fibers waiting to show off, waiting to be fed that elixir of life, blood. In fact, your body is literally bristling with these stout fibers, packed in like sardines just under the surface, all clamoring every time you lift an arm or leg for an opportunity to show you what you're made of. And one of their most insistent pleas is to be taken seriously; because if you do, they rightfully claim, if you give them a few serious efforts, they will give you the literally—physically *and mentally*—empowering gift of physical strength.

- Through exercise your physical and mental powers begin to work in tandem, a lot like the arrangement of a bicycle built for two. Your mind marshals your muscles and breathing and adrenaline so that your body can act to increase physical health and strength; this done, your body has made your mind feel fresher, more ambitious, and better protected from both outside dangers and disease. With the bicycle built for two the front rider does most of the steering, while the back rider is mainly an additional power source. However, their combined efforts can result in a smooth ride at high speeds with a less than gut-wrenching exertion. And while it is true that a person's brain can perform very well without a vigorous body supporting it, yet, like the lone cyclist straining up a hill, what is the point when it is possible to reach the same destination over flat land with four legs pumping the pedals.

Part 5: Thriving in the Single Life (in Splendid Solitude)

• Gives you all-around power. Exercise provides a measure of physical power, everyone knows that. And, as I have suggested already, it can enhance mental powers. But how exactly does exercise affect the mind? Does it make you smarter? If cleaning the mind of its recent accumulation of dusty worries, and ordering small confusions means making you smarter then it makes you smarter. However I believe this enhancement lies more in the way decisions are made, in the way business and life are likely to be carried on. That is, more positively, cheerfully, humorously—in short in a happy confident pleasant manner that can't help giving people you deal with the impression you are a winner.

And now I think it is only fitting that I bring this final Part about thriving solo to a close with a tribute to the grand master of happy independent living.

66.

Get a Cat to Learn How to be Alone

※

Far from being the last refuge of relationship-starved older women—which by the way is a myth—cats are healthy companions for one between relationships. And, happily, they are just as agreeable to be around when in a relationship (that is when you are involved with somebody; when they are it's admittedly too noisy), so you don't have to get rid of them when you meet somebody. However, a cat has a more important role than as companion. For though a cat may not be reliable company, not always at your side like a dog or a highly dependent spouse, a cat is always teaching, and by example at that, how to be alone. (So even if you can't bring yourself to like cats, at least read this section to learn their secrets of success.)

Cats, from the domestic to the tiger but excluding the African lion, are rugged independents. They only come together with the opposite sex for mating purposes, never even stopping by for a chat, or on the male's part looking in on the offspring. It would be hard to view this as admirable behavior in humans, especially the lack of interest by the male in his little ones. However even in this the coldest side of cats some of the noble qualities of independence shine out. The ability of the female to feed, shelter, and prepare for adulthood multiple young without assistance of any kind, for instance. This takes an admirable persistence and indeed resourcefulness which is not the less admirable because it is the outcome of animal instinct.

However, it is for less obviously heroic activities that we should admire our domestic cats. For a start, they are highly and quickly adaptable. If a cat unexpectedly has to stay out all night, or in all day, it quickly reconciles itself to the situation and in a brief time behaves as if it has

Part 5: Thriving in the Single Life (in Splendid Solitude)

never lived otherwise. Like their wonderfully flexible backs, which allow them to always right themselves and touch down from a fall feet first, the cat is ever able to take adverse circumstances and treat them as if they were ideal circumstances. If someone takes away their sleeping basket and locks them in a bare kitchen, they will plop down on the counter top and get a full night's rest; if they get soaked in a sudden downpour they, once inside, will immediately set to work on their wet coat with an enthusiasm which suggests they consider their state mainly a great opportunity for a thorough tongue washing.

Here are a few of the feline attributes I consider most worthy of admiration and emulation:

- Cats are friendly yet politely aloof, allowing their companion to pursue their own activities most of the time, even when in contact with them.

- They perceive everything that is going on in the room continually until, as soon as their alertness begins to flag, they go to sleep.

- They are playful at least once a day, even when advanced in age.

- They scrupulously take care of themselves in regard to hygiene, food, and rest.

- They love being outdoors, smelling the scents in the wind, getting warm in the sun, using their muscles for what they were designed for: taking a sudden sprint across the yard on the pretext of some minor noise, running up a tree trunk, jumping from roof to roof.

- They are constant in all these behaviors, they do not have feline equivalents of such negative human acts and emotions as depression, self-hatred, giving up, self-destruction, apathy, world-weariness.

Happy Between Relationships

- At the same time, however, they retain most of the positive attitudes and acts, such as concern (cats will become agitated if you begin to cry and come to you), affection (rubbing against your leg, butting you with their heads), and a general happiness from simple pleasures and fulfillments, expressed in purrhaps the most purrfect sound of delight in all of nature: the purr.

(Note: you might leave running up tree trunks, roof jumping, rubbing against legs and head-butting to the feline set, and substitute a more normal human sporting activity.)

The benefits of being exposed regularly to a purr

Now let me make it clear right away that I am not suggesting that you sit there of an evening making purrs of contentment either solo or in response to a happy cat. And yet how wonderful if we could! I believe that, from a happiness point of view, human purring would be as beneficial as, from a transportation point of view, unassisted human flight would be. If actions influence moods and attitudes, as in clinical experiments where participants reported an improved mood after a session of forced smiling, imagine what the purr would do for us. A smile is one thing, a beautiful thing suggesting happiness in any of its non-twisted forms; and yet it is oftentimes shallow or brief in its pleasedness and usually mixed in its meaning. Sometimes a smile even expresses nothing but an emotion opposite to happiness—as in a sad smile, while still giving the appearance of pleasedness. A purr on the other hand is pure delight, can be sustained continuously for a large chunk of an hour, is audible and delightful to hear and so would be delighted in on top of expressing delight, which would double and augment delight.... In short it's a doggone (catgone?) shame that we do not have this feline talent.

But we still have access to cats. Like the Greyhound bus lines, cats, in gratitude for all that you have done for them, gladly offer to "leave the purring to us." Think of being a good cat owner in the same way you think of paying your utilities bill. If you do your part you will get a ready supply of heat and light: the heat being the irresistible sound of happy contentment, the light being the sight of a fellow creature living

Part 5: Thriving in the Single Life (in Splendid Solitude)
alone in happy contentment!

Commencement

Other books may conclude but how could this one? After all, since happiness need never conclude, since it need never even take a dismal hiatus between relationships, what's stopping *Happy Between Relationships* from continuing? It must and it will, in two respects.

First of all and foremost it must continue with your use of the ideas in this book as a launching pad to the creation of scads of original ways to build independent happiness.

Second, I am not finished, on the contrary I have just begun, to write on the subject of solo happiness, success, prosperity.

Thus it is far more appropriate to think of this end as merely the beginning of our relationship—one that we need never be between for long. And happily that condition is now no longer scary to either of us anyway! Because we now can:

- leave behind past relationships, realizing there were faults on both sides, and using any nagging aspects of its ending to boost our takeoff into the single life;

- see clearly what happiness is, how accessible it is to most everybody, and what must be done so as to keep it powering our lives toward success of every kind;

- look at the single life and see a bright side, in fact the many sides of a multi-faceted gemstone sparkling in the sun;

- in fact see the time between relationships as an opportunity to build a better Self—to become more knowledgeable, skilled, creative, successful, philosophical, and generally more interesting to ourselves and others.

Commencement

As I mentioned, neither you nor I are done with the crucial subject of learning to glory in the world by oneself. Neither of us knows it all. For the best success of our mutual purpose I would like your help. First please write, call, e-mail, or fax me a note as to how what you've learned in this book has helped. Second I would like to learn from you.

Write to me about your original ways of building independent happiness. If I use them in future books I will give you full credit right in the main text.

Good-bye for now, and I hope to hear from you soon!

Order Form

✸ Fax orders: (408) 873-7633

✸ Telephone orders: (408) 255-3724 Have your Visa or MasterCard ready.

✸ On-line orders: macal@pacbell.net

✸ Postal orders: McAlpine Press, Ken Rutkowski, 21265 Stevens Creek Blvd, Suite 205-527, Cupertino, CA 95014-8A

Please send me additional copies of Happy Between Relationships:
I understand that I may return the books for a full refund—for any reason, no questions asked.
Number of copies: _____

❏ Please send the *Single Life* <u>electronic</u> newsletter to me Free.
E-mail address: _____

Name: _____
Address: _____
City: _____ State: _____ Zip: _____
Telephone: (__) _____

Sales Tax: Please add 8.25% for books shipped to California addresses.
Shipping: $4.00 for first book and $2.00 for each additional.

Payment: ❏ Cheque ❏ Credit card: ❏ VISA ❏ MasterCard
Card number: _____
Name on card: _____ Exp. date: _____ / _____